Roadmap to Navigating Your Child's Disability

(Your Cheat Sheet to Advocacy, Accommodations, IEPs, 504s and everything in between)

By Chrissie Kahan

ISBN 10: 0-9979333-4-8
ISBN 13: 978-0-9979333-4-5
Publisher: King Kahan Publishing, LLC

Dedication

To Kelly, Karyn and Nanette.
Thank you for offering me your perspective as
I created this resource! I'm in awe of the way you have and
continue to be your children's biggest advocates in
navigating their disabilities.

About the Author

Chrissie Kahan has been an educator for thirteen years and an elementary assistant principal for the past eight years. As an assistant principal, one of her job responsibilities has been to be the IEP (Individualized Education Plan) and SST (Student Support Team) Chair who facilitates meetings for students with disabilities. As the facilitator of these meetings, she has a multitude of responsibilities that include working collaboratively with all school personnel and families to ensure each child is getting appropriate accommodations, along with making sure that each document is compliant within the legal outlined timelines. But most importantly, she has had to ensure that every person around the team table is working together in the best interest of each child. Chrissie is also certified in the area of education and a passionate advocate for ALL students. She wanted to create a comprehensive resource where any parent could easily and in a clear, concise manner find the information they needed to understand the process within the public education system in order to best help their child to get the appropriate services needed for their disability.

Introduction

Trying to determine if your child has a disability, getting the actual diagnosis, and then knowing how to help your child in this day and age can be an exhausting, overwhelming struggle for any parent. Even just trying to research the topic can bring up an abundance of resources that takes time, effort, and a knowledge of jargon that you may not have to determine if those resources are even helpful. Reaching out to your child's school for support can also bring about a mixed reaction that may not leave you with the supportive feeling you are looking for. As much as I have loved being a teacher and educator, we too often are growing in our own understanding of disability awareness.

Your job as a parent is the most important in the world. You deserve a comprehensive resource that gives you all the information you need and allows you access to me, your own personal advocate who helps you…to help your child without having to pay outside educational advocates, law consultants, psychologists, attorneys, etc.

As an educator for the past thirteen years, certified in Special Education, an IEP (Individualized Education Program) and SST (Student Support Team) chair, and an avid advocate for ALL students, I want your child to be celebrated for his/her uniqueness by getting the type of support needed along with you also feeling like you're a partner in the process.

And although I have been unable to have children of my own (see my other book Navigating the Road of Infertility), for five amazing months I was a mom attempting to adopt two girls, ages 5 and 7, who each had their own disabilities: ADHD, PTSD and a sensory processing disorder. Within those five months my whole life revolved around the care of those two young girls who needed constant intervention, therapeutic support and behavior management at home. I too sat on the other side of the team table and my professional experience did not diminish the anguish it was to hear a team of people talk about your most precious baby. It was only then that I realized the thankless, tireless struggle parents go through at home trying to support their child in managing their child's disability. So I want you to know you are not alone.

Welcome to your personal "Roadmap to Navigating Your Child's Disability!" Let me be your guide and advocate to help make at least one aspect of the most influential job of being a parent a little easier.

Contents

Part I: Cracking the Code of Educational Jargon

IEP, SST, 504, ESL, SLD, wtf, lol.

OK, so the last two aren't actual educational terms. I threw them in though because that's how all the educational acronyms can make you feel, like you're having a conversation in a warped text language where you never learned the vocabulary. If you feel clueless when educators start breaking out these terms, but don't want to seem like you're clueless, you are not alone!

Educational lingo changes all the time. Sometimes even faster than educators themselves can keep up with it. I remember being a new teacher and having no idea what some of the terminology meant. But I didn't want to seem stupid or unknowledgeable, so I would nod my head smiling in agreement, all the while pretending to understand the terms. Later, I would look up the vocabulary on my own. In a school setting, we are inundated with these terms. So much so that sometimes we don't realize how much we are talking in these acronyms. Other times, we are inwardly so proud of the fact we learned all these terms, we can't wait to spew out our newfound vocabulary in conversation so others will hear this newfound knowledge and revel at how well we cracked the educational code. Either way, you as the parent have every right to stop an educator and ask them to explain a definition or process if you don't fully understand it. If you feel shy in doing that, I've broken down the terms below in ways that actual human beings can understand without needing multiple resources. Just know you are not alone in feeling like the educational terminology is like getting a bad hand in Scrabble.

Educational Jargon Cheat Sheet:

IDEA:

It all starts with IDEA. You are probably reading that as idea but it is pronounced I.D.E.A. and it is the most important law that was passed in 2004. It stands for The Individuals with Disabilities Education Act and it outlines a whole lot of criteria that need to be followed for kids ages 3-21 whether they have a disability or one is suspected. The bottom line is this law makes advocacy possible because it levels the playing field by outlining how public agencies need to provide early intervention, special education and related services to more than eligible infants, toddlers, children, and youth with disabilities.

ADA:

This stands for the Americans with Disabilities Act. It is a Civil Rights law that is intended to prevent discrimination solely on the basis of disability in employment, public services, and for accommodations.

504:

We will talk about the specific terminology of a 504 plan below, but the gist of the 504 is that it is also a Civil

Rights law that is supposed to prevent discrimination of one's disability in programs and services.

*A great resource that breaks down the comparison of ADA, IDEA, and Section 504 can be found at dredf.org

Infants and Toddlers:

This is the first step in early intervention services. Prior to your child being school aged (age 5), there are services they can get through the public school system. If you suspect they have a delay with talking, walking, life skills, etc. look up the process within your county. It can usually be found under the special education section for the public school system. With infants and toddlers, once you make the request, they will do the testing, and if your child qualifies, services will be provided in your home.

Child Find:

This is what it's called in my county but it may be different in your school district. This is for preschool or prekindergarten children along with those kids in a district who may be going to a private school. If your child meets that criteria, you call the identified office number. Again, look on your district's Special Education portion of the website to find this. Then you call and make the referral. That office will then contact the home school in your area. They will schedule a meeting with you to hear the concerns and recommend any testing. As the parent or guardian,

you will have to bring the child to the school for testing. Then, you may have to bring them to that location as well to receive services.

SST:

This stands for Student Support Team. If there is a concern that you or the school has, this is normally the first type of formal meeting called. It is different than a conference because you will have a team of people from the school. This can include the student support team chair who facilitates the meeting, classroom teacher(s), special educator(s), the guidance counselor, the nurse, and/or the psychologist. At times, the reading specialist is also there. If that seems like an overwhelming amount of people, you are not alone in thinking that. Just remember everyone is there to SUPPORT your child which means you as well. Ultimately, the team members should have a helpful demeanor and will offer suggestions on appropriate next steps to better help your child in the area identified as an issue. This team can meet for concerns in the following areas: social, emotional, inattention, academic, medical, and attendance. You may request this type of meeting if you have a concern in one of these areas.

504 plan:

The 504 plan refers to section 504 of the Rehabilitation Act and the Americans with Disabilities Act (ADA). This basically means that while your child does not qualify for an IEP, he/she is entitled to accommodations to help them be successful in the school environment due to the disability. The disability can include ADD, Anxiety, Cystic Fibrosis, and/or any other documented disability. This plan would be most appropriate if your child is not significantly below grade level (1-2 years) but have a disability which is impacting them educationally where they need accommodations like reduced distractions, extended time, repetition of directions, chunking of assignments, etc. to be successful in school.

IEP:

This stands for Individualized Education Plan. When a child has been found to have a disability that is causing a significant educational impact, they can qualify for this type of plan. This means that the child is at least 1-2 years below grade level, their disability is causing a negative educational impact and they require specially designed instruction through this lengthy plan. The plan will include goals that match up to their areas of need based on their disability with objectives included for how those goals will be met. A case manager will be assigned to monitor and implement this plan for the child. The IEP team which should include you the parent needs to meet at least once a year to review and update this document.

FBA:

FBA stands for a Functional Behavioral Assessment. A team will recommend and get permission from you the guardian for this type of assessment if they would like to understand specific behaviors from a child. It includes a variety of assessment methods: observations, interviews with teachers, parents, review of referrals for behavior, etc. that allow the team to analyze the child's (problem behaviors) to determine what is triggering those behaviors and what function they are serving for the child. I have never met a child who willingly wants to display "bad" behaviors. They just may not know how to appropriately express how they're feeling. The goal of this type of assessment is to help the team get a better understanding of when these behaviors are happening so they can develop a plan to help the child learn replacement behaviors.

BIP:

The BIP is the next step after the FBA as it is the actual Behavior Intervention Plan. Normally this type of document is developed through the team with input from the psychologist, special educator, and teachers to focus on 1-2 problem behaviors for the child. There is usually a plan of positive incentives put in place (i.e., some kind of reward for the positive behavior) in order to get the child to the identified behavior the team wants instead of the problem behavior. There also may be training listed for staff who will help work with the child along with a response plan (what the school will do if the child becomes violent, runs out of school, or is destructive to property). As the parent or guardian, you should always be aware and sign off on the plan before it is implemented as it is a formal assessment measure. We will talk more about that in Part II.

AT:

Assistive Technology

For this definition we are going to specifically look at how it is defined throughout special education in schools. It is any item, piece of equipment or system that is used to increase, maintain, or improve the functional capabilities of children with disabilities.

Examples (Audio Recorders, F/M systems that amplify sound for students with hearing issues)

Schools usually have their own assistive technology department within the county. If you have questions about what is available for your child, reach out to your school's IEP chair or Special Education department chair to ask who you should contact about the types of available assistive technology within that county.

PLAAFP:

This is a specific section that is required on every IEP called the Present Levels of Academic Achievement and Functional Performance. Basically, for every area the team is saying is affected by your child's disability, they need to show data as to why your child is performing below level in that area of need to

determine that they need a goal to help support them due to their disability.

ESY:

This stands for Extended School Year and is a page specifically on the IEP. Extended School Year is Special Education summer school. In order for your child to qualify for this, the team will review the questions on this specific page. Normally, they are looking at data that shows your child regresses with skills learned over a break. Extended School Year can be very helpful for students who tend to not retain learned skills and/or who continue to benefit from the school structure over the summer.

LRE:

This acronym is normally thrown out on the last page of an IEP after the team has gone through all of the other services. It stands for Least Restrictive Environment which in layman's terms means that your child is in the right classroom setting to receive the services. Normally the team has to list the settings they have considered. The first is always general education without accommodations and supports. This means your child in the classroom with no accommodations. The second is general education with supports and accommodations. This should be the next environment considered when your child has an IEP as they will need accommodations to be successful with their plan. After that, if their IEP has been tried and the child is not successful, you may see OGE (Outside General Education) hours. This could mean your child needs an interventional reading program outside of the classroom with the reading specialist or the special educator. On this page if your child has speech services, you will also see that they are out of the general education environment for that. Outside general education could also reference a self-contained program or placement. A self-contained placement means a different regional program for your child. We will discuss this in more detail in Part II.

FAPE:
This is a popular term and it stands for "Free Appropriate Public Education." One of my favorite links: understood.org breaks it down by each letter. F: Free means that all students with disabilities will be educated at the public school's expense. A: Appropriate means that your child will have a specific program that is tailored to their needs. This plan is outlined in their IEP.

P: Public refers to the public school system. Children no matter the nature and severity of their disabilities have the right to be educated under the public school system. E: Education must be provided to every school aged child with a disability. This education should be outlined according to your child's plan and should prepare them for their future including further education, employment and independent living.

So basically it means your child is getting what they need within their school setting.

FERPA:
Family Educational Rights and Privacy Act of 1974 is federal legislation in the United States that protects student's personally identifiable information. This Act states that parents of students under 18 or students over 18 be allowed to view and propose changes to their educational record. The act also states that the school must have a signed release from that parent or eligible student in order to release the personally identifiable information to anyone. This is usually done through a document called a release of records.

You may also have lettered acronyms thrown at you in relation to the titles of school personnel which can seem confusing. Refer to the list below anytime to help understand the role associated with each acronym.

IEP Chair: They run the IEP meetings. If you have a concern about meeting notes or your child's services, they along with the case manager are the ones to contact.

SLP: Speech Language Pathologist: They service students who have speech and language concerns. This includes articulation, stuttering, communication, pragmatics, and language. If there is a concern with your child in any of the listed areas, they should be included in the meeting.

OT: Occupational Therapist: Occupational therapy is a health profession where therapists help individuals engage and perform duties in their daily life. In the school setting for students who qualify for occupational therapy, they can work with the student on a range of things including visual (hand eye coordination) and gross motor skills (the ability to control the large muscles of the body for sitting, crawling, walking, running, handwriting, and other activities.)

PT: Physical Therapist: A physical therapist is a member of the school's team if a child qualifies for services on their IEP based on their needs. The school based physical therapist promotes motor development (the growth of muscular coordination with a child) and the student's participation through everyday routines and activities. They design and perform therapeutic interventions that focus on functional mobility for the student.

ESOL/ELL/ESL: These are all acronyms that stand for English as a Second Language. There is usually an ESOL teacher assigned to every school, although they may have multiple schools depending on the identified population of students who have English as a second language that attend the school. This teacher is there to provide instruction for these students on learning English. They also can be a resource to teachers and the community to provide suggestions for interventions that can help English Language Learning students become successful.

Each school district also has outside general education self-contained settings. That means that your child would not be in a regular "inclusion" classroom where they were included with peers that did not have an IEP. These self-contained settings also tend to have acronyms. While the acronyms may change depending on your district, I wanted you to have a basic understanding of the descriptions of the types of programs that can be offered.

ECLS: Early Childhood Learning Support
These are programs that meet the needs of preschool and pre-kindergarten students with IEP's. These services are in a structured environment where positive behavior strategies, use of developmentally appropriate practices, social skills, and a multi-sensory approach to learning is used within the school environment.

FALS: Functional Academic Learning Support
This type of program is for students in need of functional academic learning support who show significant delays in intelligence, adaptive functioning, communication, and academic

functioning. Teachers within this type of learning environment will use a functional life skills curriculum with focuses on personal management, community, recreation/leisure, career/vocational, and decision making. Learning materials are extremely modified in this setting.

CALS: Communication and Learning Support
Communication and learning support services are for those students who have complex communication, socialization, and learning needs as a result of having been diagnosed with Autism. Students within these types of programs usually have identified and significant delays in the areas of cognition, communication, social/emotional, and adaptive behavior.

BLS: Behavioral and Learning Support
If a student is assigned to this type of service delivery program, it means that they have significant social, emotional, behavioral, and learning needs that need to be met in a self-contained (outside general education) setting. These students typically have average intelligence but may not be achieving due to their complex social, emotional and behavior needs.

In Part III: Disabilities from A-Z, we will take a look at the most common identified disabilities for students in public education. However, some are acronyms that require them to be added to our educational cheat sheet. Check them out below:

SLD: This stands for Specific Learning Disability.
This type of disability may impact the child in understanding or using language (spoken or written) and may show itself in their ability to listen, think, read, speak, write, spell, or do mathematical calculations. It includes conditions such as perceptual disabilities (the way information enters the brain), minimal brain dysfunction (a neurodevelopmental disorder found in 20% of school aged children characterized by evidences of immaturity involving control of activities, emotions and behavior along with deficits in communicating skills in reading, writing and mathematics), dyslexia (disorder that involves difficulty with learning to read or interpret words, letters or other symbols but do not effect general intelligence), and developmental aphasia (a communication disorder that results from damage to the parts of the brain that contain language; may cause difficulties in speaking, writing, listening and reading but does not affect intelligence.)

TBI: Traumatic Brain Injury
This is a specific injury to the brain, caused by an external force (such as an accident), that results in total or partial functional disability (any loss of function for any organ, body part or system) or psychosocial (development of the personality) impairment, or both that negatively affects a student's educational performance. Injury to the brain is different from an injury to other parts of our body. No two brain

injuries are alike. A person who has a brain injury due to open or closed head injuries can have one or more areas affected: Cognition, Language, Memory, Attention, Reasoning, Abstract Thinking, Judgment, Problem Solving, Sensory, Perceptual and Motor abilities, Psychosocial behavior, Physical functions, Information Processing, and Speech. These type of brain injuries are different than brain injuries that are caused by birth trauma or are congenital. The student with this injury had a normal brain and then due to whatever happened to them caused the head trauma that had their brain injured.

OHI: Other Health Impairment

Having a disability caused by disease, condition, injury or disorder that affects vitality, strength, and alertness. This results in a student having limited alertness in the educational environment thus negatively affecting their educational performance. Other Health Impairment can include the following: Asthma, ADD/ADHD (Attention Deficit Disorder or Attention Deficit Hyperactivity Disorder), Diabetes, Cystic Fibrosis, Epilepsy, a heart condition, Cancer, Hemophilia, Lead poisoning, Nephritis, Rheumatic fever, Sickle cell anemia or Tourette Syndrome. If your child is diagnosed with another medical condition that is not listed above and is negatively impacting their ability to perform in the classroom, then it also may be considered under this disability category.

PDD-NOS: Pervasive Developmental Disorder-Not Otherwise Specified

This category is used to refer to children who have significant problems with communication and play, and some difficulty interacting with others, but are too social to be considered autistic. It is sometimes referred to as a milder form of Autism.

Twice Exceptional (2es):

Of course we all consider our children to be exceptional, so this term can throw us all off because who wouldn't want their child to be twice the amount of what is considered exceptional. What it really means though is a child who has above average intelligence along with a disability. You could say they qualify for the gifted or advanced academics program in school, but they also have a disability. They should not be unable to participate in the school program for advanced learners due to their disability, but we will get into that more in Part III.

Ok, that was a lot of lingo. Take a deep breath as we continue on in our navigation below. Before we journey to Part II, there are several more terms of clarification needed. And let me tell you a secret: often some educators may not know the difference between these three. However, as a parent it is really important that you do, so you know how to best help your child be successful in school. When I'm trying to show the differences between each, I refer to a chart resource

I found at gpb.org to break down the definition, and examples of each.

Strategy: A loosely defined collective term that is often used interchangeable with the word "intervention"' however, strategies are usually just considered effective instructional practices and/or good classroom instruction for all students.

Intervention: An intervention should be targeted (specific) instruction that is based on an individual student's needs. Strategies can become interventions if the strategy includes a step by step description on how it will be put in place and by who. Teachers are starting specific interventions for your child, if they put them on a personalized behavior point sheet, have them begin to work with the reading specialist or have them go out for any kind of reading program.

Accommodation: This is a specific change made to the classroom environment for testing or during instruction. By giving a child who needs this type of change, you are "leveling the playing field" which means giving them equal access to the instruction that is being taught by changing the approach to meet their needs due to their disability. In Part III, we will talk about the best accommodations for each disability in school, but until then, here are some general examples:

- Preferential seating (seated near the teacher or closest to instruction)
- Use of a word bank for a test
- Small group testing
- Extended time for assignments and/or tests
- Provided with an extra set of books at home

Modification: This is a change in WHAT the student is expected to learn or show that they have learned. This is usually only put in place for students that have an IEP since in order to qualify for that IEP they are significantly (1-2 years) below grade level. It means that they are still working on the same subject of the content (Reading, Math, S.S., Science, etc.) but that the course content has to be changed to reduce their learning expectations. An example could be in the area of math where grade level peers without an IEP are expected to learn multiplication and division, while the child with the IEP is only expected to meet the objectives on their IEP in that area such as counting to 100.

Part II: TEAM

What is it? What are the timelines?
And how do I advocate respectfully for my child?

When you hear the word team, you tend to automatically think about a sports team. Yet, this is the term that is often referred to especially in the elementary setting for school support staff such as the facilitator of the meeting, teacher(s), the school nurse, the guidance counselor, the school psychologist, and any other related service staff to sit along with you the parent or guardian to work together as a TEAM on how to best support the needs of your child.

Depending on the school system and school setting, team can occur in a variety of ways. You can request a team as a parent (preferably in writing) and the school should schedule this within a reasonable time period, normally within 30 days of the request. Or the school will request a team meeting. If the school requests it, then usually the secretary will call to confirm an available date and time with you the parent or guardian, tell you the purpose of the meeting, and will mail out a written notification of the meeting. This is so you have a clear understanding of the purpose along with who will be there. A team is different from a conference.

I will give you some hints so you can recognize if a school is considering requesting a team for your child. Is the teacher commenting on their ability to stay focused during class, stay seated more, or wondering why they need constant breaks, along with asking you if they need breaks at home? Have you heard that your child is not progressing at the same level as other children their age or that they are talkative, have difficulty getting along with other students, or have such an independent, unique personality? If one or more of these things has been said to you in a professional, teacher way, chances are the school will be considering what is called a Student Support team meeting where with you along with other school staff will meet to discuss how to put interventions in place to help your child in the school setting.

So what is a SST (Student Support Team)? As much as I wish all educational settings truly understood and followed the implied conclusion to the term Student Support Team, some do not which is why I want you to know that no matter what the concerning area is whether it be emotional, academic, social, health, attendance, etc. the school should want to work with you to help SUPPORT your child not reprimand you or your child. This type of team may also have a different acronym in your state such as (School Study Team or Student Intervention Team). But the most important take away is that this type of team is made up of school staff along with you in collaboration to help your child. You should never feel as though your child is being ostracized or that you are only hearing negative things. We will talk more about respectful advocacy later in this chapter so you know how to convey your feelings in a professional way if anyone on the team makes you feel like this.

For this type of meeting, you should know what the purpose will be along with the staff members who will be there prior to the meeting taking place. If you do not and feel uncomfortable walking into this meeting, call the secretary and ask to speak to the person who runs these meetings to get your questions answered about of the purpose of the meeting and who will be there. At this meeting, staff members along with you will have the opportunity to share your child's progress including any concerns they may have in order to develop interventions for your child. An instructional intervention is a plan or a set of steps that will help the child improve in the area of need identified.

What you need to know about any intervention is that it should be:

Intentional (aimed at your child's specific weakness or area of concern)

Specific and formalized (should be outlined for a specific amount of time and done consistently)
We normally tell educators that an intervention should be done consistently and monitored over 4-6 weeks before it is determined to be effective or not

Set up in a way that you and the school can monitor how well the intervention is working

It is important to continue to understand that an intervention is different from a strategy or an accommodation and modification as I outlined at the end of Part I.

After the initial meeting, the school should be monitoring whether the interventions are successful. They may even put this onto an informal type of plan. In my county, this is called a Student Support Plan, and it has specific goals and identified interventions on it. The team should meet to update these goals with you in attendance. No matter what the procedure is within your child's school system, you will want a follow-up meeting to review your child's progress. Remember, this should be at least 4-6 weeks after the meeting to measure your child's progress adequately.

Most times, especially if there are attentional concerns and ADD is suspected, the team will request checklists to be done. There are a couple of checklists that could be requested: Conners and Vanderbilt. These are diagnostic tools (rating scales) that will be filled out by you the parent and the teachers. The results will then be sent home to you and/or explained at a team meeting usually by the nurse or psychologist to be shared with the pediatrician. If your child is diagnosed with ADD by the pediatrician, remember it is ALWAYS your decision alone as the parent to decide to medicate your child. Whether or not your child requires medication, if your child has a documented disability and requires accommodations in order for them to be successful in a school setting, the school could develop a more involved plan for them. Determining whether the plan will be a 504 plan or an IEP requires the team to understand how significant the child's disability is impacting them in the school setting. If the child is significantly below grade level as in 1-2 years and it could be because of their disability, or if their disability is having a negative educational impact where they need more specialized instruction then most likely the team will proceed or you should request an IEP meeting. If the child is on grade level, but is still having a negative impact within school due to their disability, then a 504 plan could be considered.

The results of the Vanderbilt checklists can seem overwhelming. Here is what you can expect: a packet of all of the rating scales along with a form letter in the front. The form letter will outline the number of people needed in each area to show that there are characteristics for ADD, ADHD, Anxiety, or Depression.

A 504 plan will have different sections to it. It is still considered a legal document because of section 504 which states that written education plans are required for all students who are disabled under Section 504 of the Rehabilitation Act of 1973. Each 504 plan should include a description of why the child is eligible for those services. This usually includes the diagnosis, description of diagnosis, areas that the disability impacts, and any supporting documentation (report cards, formal assessments, parent and teacher report) of how that disability impacts them followed by if the team thinks that the disability impacts them adversely in the educational setting (the answer should be yes for a student to qualify). That section is usually called the 504 Eligibility page. The next section is a full list of the types of accommodations that child needs to be successful in the classroom and during testing along with a description of who will be implementing those accommodations and where the accommodations will be implemented. Because you typically want your child to have these accommodations throughout the school, as the chair of these meetings, I usually type in "classroom teachers" or "school staff" as the people responsible and "school" for the setting. Again, this is a legal document that must be followed and you as an important member of the team have a right to review to amend as needed.

If interventions have been tried for the appropriate amount of time and your child's education is still being negatively impacted, the team may move to the IEP (Individualized Education Plan) process. In general though, if your child already has a 504 plan, the team will want to monitor that for at least a year to determine if the plan is making a positive impact. If the 504 plan is not helping your child meet with success, a team could move to an IEP team meeting which I always tell parents is just the same staff members with a different name and more paperwork.

In order for your child to qualify for this type of plan (IEP) it would mean the answer is yes to these questions: your child is significantly below grade level 1-2 years, your child's education is being negatively impacted, and your child requires specially designed instruction. The team has to use the informal assessments (interventions they have already done combined with daily performance) along with getting additional information in order to determine if your child qualifies. We will go through the IEP process below in more detail.

STEP 1: REFERRAL

If you have been following the steps above then it is more than likely the SST will move forward with a referral to the IEP team (again usually it is the same people, just more paperwork and a different name of the meeting). If not, and you have read the questions above and determined that your child may be in need of an IEP, you can always make your own written referral to your child's school. Make sure you include in writing: your name, the date, the fact that you suspect your child has a disability, and are requesting

an IEP team. The school should schedule that team within 30 days of your request.

STEP 2: ASSESSMENT

The next step of this process is assessment. Like I said, if you have been following the process of going through SST, the team already has some informal assessment data to refer to. If you have not gone through SST or any prior meeting, then there is still informal assessment data to refer to which can be any report such as report card comments, grades, tests, or state assessment (test) scores the child has along with teacher observations. The team will also want to do more formalized testing in the form of specific assessments done through the special educator, psychologist, and the guidance counselor who usually observes in the classroom. If there are any communication issues, the speech therapist may also want to do testing. That same idea is true if the child has any fine motor or gross motor concerns with the occupational therapist. These assessments are outlined at the IEP team meeting, and the people who will be assessing your child should tell you the type of assessment they will be doing. If you have questions about the type of assessment, the name of the assessment, or want to ask for a specific type of testing to be done, this is your time to do so. The team will need you to sign for permission to move forward with these tests. Then the team has 60 days to complete them (this if for an Initial Evaluation of a student). When a team is reevaluating whether a child qualifies for services, they have 90 days to complete assessments. In team notes called (Prior Written Notice) which gives you a summary of everything discussed at the meeting, the team should also share the disability they suspect and are testing for.

Here is a list of some formal assessments the team may want to complete if your child has been referred to the IEP team along with the purpose for them.

Educational Testing: To determine your child's educational levels.
YCAT: The Young Children's Achievement Test yields an overall Early Achievement standard score and individual subtest standard scores in the areas of General Information, Reading, Writing, Mathematics, and Spoken Language. It is usually given to students aged 4-7 within the school setting.

*This report is usually a lot shorter than the WJIV and it is equally important to pay attention to the chart given with the different subtests, scores, percentile rank, and age equivalent for your child along with the summary at the end.

WJIV: Woodcock Johnson IV: a diagnostic tool that can be used from age 2 on and ranged from Kindergarten to the end of college. There are three forms of this type of test: achievement battery form A, form B, and

form C. There are 11 subtests in each. The special educator using the assessment will use what is called a Qualitative Observation to determine how typical or atypical your child's answers were on the tasks in each subgroup.

There are six cluster scores in Reading for this test. The subtests consist of the ones listed below:
→ **Reading:** Letter Word Identification and Passage Comprehension
→ **Broad Reading:** Letter Word Identification, Passage Comprehension, and Sentence Reading Fluency
→ **Basic Reading:** Letter Word Identification and Word Attack
→ **Reading Comprehension:** Passage Comprehension, Reading Recall, and Reading Vocabulary
→ **Reading Fluency:** Oral Reading and Sentence Reading Fluency
Reading Rate
Sentence Reading Fluency
Word Reading Fluency

Four cluster scores can be obtained for Math:
→ **Mathematics:** Applied Problems and Calculation
→ **Broad Mathematics:** Applied Problems, Calculation, and Math Facts Fluency
→ **Math Calculation:** Calculation and Math Facts Fluency

→**Math Problem Solving:** Applied Problems and Number Matrices

In Writing, four cluster scores can also be obtained:
→**Written Language:** Spelling and Writing Samples
→**Broad Written Language:** Spelling, Writing Samples, and Sentence Writing Fluency
→**Basic Writing Skills:** Spelling and Editing
→**Written Expression:** Writing Samples and Sentence Writing Fluency

*The most important things to look for with the WJIV are the chart that has all of the scores along with the summary at the end. It will be broken into three categories: the standard battery (this is the subtest of one of the areas above), your child's standard score, and the grade equivalent of that score.

Classroom Observation: The counselor or other identified team member will observe your child in the classroom in the targeted subject of concern to share information about the child's current performance levels.

Psychological: Cognitive Testing: To determine current cognitive levels.

WISC-IV: The Wechsler Intelligence Scale for Children is an individually administered IQ test used with children aged from 6-16. Younger children are tested using the Wechsler Preschool and Primary Scale of Intelligence called the WPPSI. There are 15 subtests on the WISC-IV, but they may or may not all be used depending on the areas of concern. Sometimes the assessments overlap with what their testing from each assessor. The subtests include:

Block Design: measuring an individual's ability to analyze and synthesize an abstract design and reproduce that design from colored plastic blocks.
Digit Span: measures short-term auditory memory and attention.

Picture Concepts: measures categorical, abstract reasoning.
Coding: measures visual-motor dexterity, associative nonverbal learning, and nonverbal short-term memory.

Vocabulary: measures the student's verbal fluency and concept formation as well as word knowledge and word usage.
Letter Number Sequencing: measures attention span, short-term auditory recall, processing speed, and sequencing abilities.
Matrix Reasoning: measures visual processing and abstract, spatial perception and may be influenced by concentration, attention and persistence.

Comprehension: measures common-sense social

knowledge, practical judgment in social situations, and level of social maturation along with the extent of the development of moral conscience.

Symbol Search: requires the student to determine whether a target symbol appears among the symbols shown in a search group.
Picture Completion: measures a student's ability to recognize familiar items and to identify missing parts.

Cancellation: measures visual vigilance/neglect, selective attention, and speed in processing visual information in accordance with previous attempts along the same line.

Information: measures general cultural knowledge, long term memory, and acquired facts.

Arithmetic: measures numerical accuracy, reasoning, and mental arithmetic ability.

Word Reasoning: measures verbal abstract reasoning requiring analogical and categorical thinking, as well as verbal concept formation and expression.

*Whew, that's a lot. This assessment is really important to get information about the child's IQ. For examples of the subtests described above visit thinktonight.com

Also, when you get this report, the scores are usually on the last page of the report. The second to last page is the summary and the introduction is always fun to read because it says what your child loves the most about school and usually what they want to be when they grow up.

WASI-II: This is still Wechsler, it is just the Wechsler Abbreviated Scale of Intelligence. You'd think that would mean the report would be shorter and/or easier to understand, but sadly it is not. It is also a general intelligence or IQ test that is designed to assess specific and overall cognitive abilities to children, adolescents and adults. It is a battery of four subtests:

- Vocabulary
- Block Design
- Similarities
- Matrix Reasoning

Psychological: Rating scales: To determine current social emotional levels.

BASC-3: This stands for the Behavior Assessment System for Children, Third Edition and is designed to measure a child's adaptive and problem behaviors in the community, school, and home settings. There are three age levels: preschool, child, and adolescent. What this means is that the teachers, parents and sometimes even the child will be given rating scales to complete. Sometimes there can be a lot of questions and you may not know how to answer, so always seek guidance from the psychologist if unclear. Ultimately though, this information is used to measure a child's strengths and weaknesses with their social-emotional levels (their ability to understand the feelings of others, control their own feelings and behaviors, and get along with peers).

ASRS: The Autism Spectrum Rating Scales are given out to parents and teachers when the team suspects that Autism could be a diagnosis. These rating scales are designed to effectively identify symptoms, behaviors and associated features of Autism Spectrum Disorders in children and adolescents aged 2 to 18.

Speech Language: To determine strengths and weaknesses with articulation or language.

GTFA-2: This stands for the Goldman-Fristoe Test of Articulation. It is used to measure a child's strengths and weaknesses with their articulation (the way they sound out letters and words). This assessment provides a wide range of information by sampling both spontaneous and imitative sound production including single words and conversational speech. It is given to kids as early as age 2.

CASL: The Comprehensive Assessment of Spoken Language is the type of test a team uses when they need to measure a child's strengths and weaknesses

with language. It provides a precise picture of language processing skills and structural knowledge which allows the team to understand the child's development in language. It is ideal for measuring delayed language, spoken language disorders, dyslexia, and aphasia.

Overwhelmed by the testing acronyms yet? Prep yourself for an overwhelming explanation of these assessments at the team meeting followed by the tedious, hard to understand reports that will follow. Hopefully the information above will provide you with some relief to tackling those reports.

STEP 3: ELIGIBILITY

The team will meet again with you within 60 days after you sign permission for the assessments. Most states and counties have a rule now that they should send home to you any type of document that will be reviewed at the team within 5 business days of the meeting. This includes the assessment reports. It is important that you get a copy of these ahead of time. I would want to in case I did not understand something in them. That way I could take a list of specific questions I wanted to ask to the meeting and/or look up or ask a friend for their input on my questions. At this meeting, the IEP team will decide whether your child has a disability based on their findings. They should then still consider the informal assessments (classroom performance on a daily basis) along with the results of the formal testing when they make their decision. They are looking for one of 14 identified disabilities that fall under IDEA when determining eligibility: Autism, Deaf-Blindness, Deafness, Developmental Delay (through age 7), Emotional Disability, Hearing Impairment, Intellectual Disability, Multiple Disabilities, Orthopedic Impairment, Other Health Impairment, Specific Learning Disability, Speech or Language Impairment, Traumatic Brain Injury, or Visual Impairment, including Blindness.

*Just know that the "assessment review" meeting will probably be one of the most boring, and long meetings that will make you feel as though you lost the ability to understand spoken language with all of the subtests, acronyms and information being thrown at you. All the information you usually need to know is found on the summary of each report, usually the last page and paragraph(s). So, don't get overwhelmed by the jargon. Also, feel free to interrupt and ask questions if you don't understand what a presenter is saying about a report. You can ask for more information about the type of subtest or to see a scale that shows where your child fell in comparison to other peers their age. As a team chair, I've tried to reduce the content presented in these meetings along with promoting graphs and other color-coded reports. However, it still tends to be very overwhelming. The most important thing is that you walk away from the meeting knowing:

- *Did your child qualify for an IEP?*
- *What was the label (code) they qualified under?*
- *When will the team be meeting again to develop the IEP?*

STEP 4: IEP DEVELOPMENT

If your child is determined to be eligible, normally an eligibility document is completed at the end of the team meeting once all assessments have been reviewed. Your signature is needed on that document as you are a very important member of the team. Another team within 30 days will then be scheduled to develop the actual plan (IEP) for your child. This is the official legal, LONG document that will describe the accommodations, modifications, and services needed to make sure your child makes progress and gets an appropriate education. It also will list the annual (yearly) goals and objectives the school staff will use to measure your child's progress. In layman's terms, it will be a long, wordy, over the head document. We will outline below though the different sections of an IEP and what you need to look for to make sure your child is getting what they need.

STEP 5: IEP IMPLEMENTATION

Once you sign for the initial IEP to be put in place, your child should be receiving the services that are listed on the IEP. Each of the people who work with your child (all teachers, special educators, any related service providers) should also have access to that plan so they know their specific responsibilities, and your child's accommodations, modifications, and supports. This is usually found in an IEP snapshot.

STEP 6: PROGRESS MONITORING

You have the right to receive an update of your child's progress on all IEP goals quarterly (one a quarter; usually at the same time as report cards). Usually this is in writing on the same page as each goal of the IEP with a date, comment, and identification of the person who wrote the comment.

STEP 7: ANNUAL REVIEW

Once your child has an IEP, the IEP team must meet at least once a year to review whether your child is making progress towards their identified goals.

STEP 8: REEVALUATION

Once your child has an IEP, a team must reevaluate their eligibility for that IEP every 3 years. This can be through informal and formal assessments again, or if the team feels they have enough data informally, they can determine your child continues to qualify for an IEP with that data. Either way, again you are an integral part of the decision and should be an active part of the team. Here are considerations to refer to when your child is up for reevaluation,

The purpose of the reevaluation is to decide:
- If your child continues to be a child with a disability.
- Your child's educational needs and present levels of academic achievement and related developmental needs.
- Whether additions or modifications to special education services are needed to help your child meet the measurable annual goals and to participate in the general curriculum.
- Whether your child continues to need special education services.

This may or may not require new tests, but your child's IEP team needs to reevaluate:
- At least once every 3 years
- Or if you or the child's teacher ask for new tests
- And before the IEP can determine your child no longer needs special education

Let's talk about something that can often be overlooked as parents tend to count on and accept what this team of professionals is telling them at the table: disagreement. You are allowed to disagree with the team's recommendations. If you do not agree with what an assessment is stating about your child, how they will be coded to qualify for an IEP, or something listed on the IEP, speak up. Share politely, calmly, and specifically what you disagree with. Give the team and the most appropriate member of the team the opportunity to explain why they are proposing that.

If you still feel you disagree after the explanation, the team should offer to document your disagreement. In my county, if this happens it is on a separate section of the notes that are filled out from the team where they specifically go through a list of questions and how the parent disagrees. Then, at the bottom there is usually a number to call that gets the Office of Special Education for that county involved so they can propose compromise or mediation. Often, parents are afraid to go to this next step because they do not want the school to retaliate against their child. Let me let you in on a little secret: schools are mostly afraid of this step as well because it now means someone else is going to be looking at their team decisions. However, that can be a really good thing because at the end of the day, team decisions should be about what is in the best interest of the child's needs. That means that both parents and teams, if they have their own agenda, must push it to the side in order to truly turn the focus back to the child and come up with a plan that is meaningful for them. As an IEP chair, I have had to go to mediation and although the process was stressful, the outcome always turned out to be positive because the parents felt heard, I had to take a hard look at team decisions which impacted my facilitation of teams and management of team members, and the outcome always benefited the child.

Sometimes you may have personalities in education who are not willing to compromise on team decisions or who come to some sort of resolution in mediation that you disagree with. There is always a next layer to that process which can end in filing a state complaint against the school. **Refer back to your Procedural Safeguards document that talks about resolving disagreements to determine the best option for you.**

Now that we have an understanding of the steps and timeline of the IEP team, let's take a look at the specific parts of the IEP. When you receive this document, you will feel as though you are buying a house with the sheer amount of paperwork. Not to mention, it is often very wordy, lengthy, and overwhelming with information, especially if you do not know what you should be looking for to understand if your child is actually getting a plan that will meet his/her needs.

The best resource I found to break down what is in an IEP is from a state resource called "Building IEPs with Maryland Families: What a Great IDEA"

What is in the IEP?

Cover Page:
This first page usually states personal information such as the student's name and address along with their disability code, the areas affected by the disability, the date of the team, and the date for reevaluation. **Look for on this page for you: make sure all of your information is up to date and correct including your email if there is a space for it.**

Eligibility:
Usually the next page will define your child's eligibility which will summarize the disability coding and the areas affected. **Look for on this page: make sure the coding of their disability is correct and all of the areas (reading, math, communication) that they need goals in are listed.**

Other Parts of the IEP will differ in their order depending on state, however, these are the portions that must be there.

A. Present Levels of Academic Achievement and Functional Performance: (PLAAFP)
No matter how this section is written in your state, it will give an overview of different data sources used to collect how your child is performing in the needed areas where the disability is affecting them. For example, let's say your child has a specific

learning disability. That is their coding. The areas of need identified are reading, math, and writing. The PLAAFP will break those down into separate sections. Within those sections, the team will show the assessment sources they used to get a picture of your child's performance. This data is used to show that your child is performing below grade level so they can qualify to have a goal in this area on their IEP. Based on the data for each section, the team determines your child's strengths and needs in order to help write the goal. **Look for on this page for you: make sure each area listed on the cover page has a section on the PLAAFP page. If the cover page says reading, math, and writing then there should be one part for reading with aligned data, strengths and needs, one part for math with aligned data, strengths and needs, and one part for writing with aligned data, strengths and needs.** There should also be a second part to the PLAAFP where the team will ask you for input about your child's educational performance and their outside of school interests. **Be honest on this part. Tell the team what you would like to see improved in your child's program.**

B. Participation in Statewide Assessments:
This is usually one to two pages on the IEP where there are a bunch of testing acronyms and sometimes aligning charts that look very confusing. All students must be included in all

state assessments to the fullest extent possible. It is important to make sure your child is aligned to receive a high school diploma. Students who would not be receiving a high school diploma, should be on an alternative track such as a self-contained program where they would also be taking statewide alternate assessments. **Look for on this page: make sure it says your child is on track to receive a diploma. Also make sure you understand if they are participating in the regular or alternative assessments. If you are not sure: ASK.**

C. Special Considerations:

This page usually focuses on communication needs. If a child receives speech and/or language services, this page is checked in a "yes" format. The team will also talk about whether they need a device to talk. If your child has a behavior intervention plan, it may also be included on this page as well along with any student who has limited English proficiency, or for a student who is blind who requires Braille. This is not usually a page that gets a lot of time spent on it.

D. Statement of Special Education and Related Services:

This is a wordy description for the section that outlines the type of services your child will be getting, who will be delivering the services, and how they will be implemented. For example, your child may have 5, 30 min. sessions inside general education with the classroom teacher, special educator, or instructional assistant. If that is the case it is important to understand that the teacher is listed first and can deliver accommodations, modifications, and other supports. All professionals listed should be in communication with one another on collecting data for your child's goals and objectives, but we will talk more about that later. If you see that your child has 2, 30 min. sessions outside of general education with the speech language pathologist, then that means that they are being taken out of the classroom to get those services. This is normal as a separate room for speech truly helps the child get the most learning with the least amount of distractions. **Look for on this page: make sure you understand the type of service, who will be implementing the service, how long they will be implementing it, and where it will be done.**

E. Supplementary Aids, Services, Program Modifications and Supports:

This page shows specific descriptions of the types of supports that will be given in the classroom along with how often they will be given and by who. The types of supports that can be listed on this page fall into one of the categories below. I've listed the categories and some examples of each for you to get a better understanding so you can go in determining what else you think your child may need.

Program Modification:

❑ Altered/modified assignments (Examples of how this can be done and listed in the discussion for this accommodation is below; a _____ indicates where your child's name would go)

- chunking of reading and assignments to ensure comprehension and avoid frustration
- delete extraneous information when possible to help _____ remain as focused as possible, and obtain the main idea
- limit the amount of visual information given on worksheets
- pair visuals with readings and vocabulary to ensure _____ understands the words/phrases being presented
- sentence starters are required to assist with _____'s ability to understand what is being asked
- fill in the blank with choices are required for questions that are open ended, short answer responses

❑ Opportunities for oral responses

- _____ requires opportunities for oral responses and extended time for the thought process in order to formulate sentences/phrases

Social/Behavior Supports:

❑ Provide frequent changes in activity or opportunities for movement

❑ Use of positive/concrete reinforcers

- _____ includes the use of positive reinforcers in the classroom. This includes but is not limited to setting behavior goals, using a chart and receiving aligned reward(s).

❑ Strategies to initiate and sustain attention

- _____ will be provided manipulatives and sensory items/strategies to promote attention to instruction.

School Personnel/Parental Supports:

❑ Adult support: (If your child requires an assistant to help assist them with attention or safety, the subjects and amount of time in the day they need that assistant will be listed here)

❑ Related service consultation (If your child is getting a consultation with OT, PT, or an SLP that is NOT listed on the services page, it will be listed here)

Instructional Supports:

❑ Allow use of manipulatives. (The discussion below should outline the specific types of manipulatives.)

❑ Have student repeat and/or paraphrase information from the board

❑ Limit amount to be copied

❑ Use of a word bank to reinforce vocabulary and/or when extended writing is required

❑ Copy of teacher/student notes

Physical/Environmental Supports:

This is for any type of change your child would need within the physical setting of the school environment due to their disability. For example:

❑ Access to an elevator

❑ Access to adaptive equipment

❑ Access to feeding devices

The two I see most in the inclusion setting are:

❑ Picture schedule

❑ Preferential seating (Discussion should include where in the room: the closest proximity to instruction and/or positive peer role models)

*Look for on this page is that for every support listed there is a specific description of how this will be implemented in the classroom, by who and for how long (daily, weekly, monthly, etc.)

F. Instructional and Testing Accommodations

Throughout this section, you will find a list along with discussion of all of the accommodations your child gets during testing. This is extremely important as this is what they will need to get during any statewide testing. The types of accommodations a child can get on testing fall into the categories below. Again, I've listed the types and some examples for your reference.

Presentation Accommodations:

• Human reader of entire test

• Human reader of selected sections of the test

• Visual cues

• Notes and outlines

*Human reader is the most common one I see under this category although in most states, students have to meet certain criteria in regards to their disability to qualify for this accommodation in the area of reading and decoding. Ask your team facilitator about those requirements if you think your child may need this.

Response Accommodations:

• Calculation devices

• Monitor test response

• Scribe

• Recording devices

• Spelling and grammar devices

• Graphic organizers

• Visual organizers

*The most common ones I see in this area are calculation devices (again we want to specify which devices/manipulatives can be used), monitor test response and scribe (someone to write or type what your child says)

Timing and Scheduling Accommodations:

- Multiple or frequent breaks
- Extended time (the amount of time your child should be given should be written in the discussion; I see 'time and a half' or 'double time' written most often. That means if everyone gets 20 minutes to test and your child has time and a half, they would get 30 minutes.
- Change Schedule or Order of Activities (Within that day or Extend over multiple days)

Setting Accommodations:

- Reduced distractions to the student
- Reduced distractions to other students

*On this page make sure you know all of the accommodations your child has access to during testing and what they mean.

G. ESY:

This page is talking about Extended School Year. Your district may have a different acronym for it, but what it means is special education summer school. The team will have to discuss whether your child qualifies for this type of summer school. Usually they are asking questions to determine if your child meets the criteria. The biggest question a team usually uses to determine if they qualify is whether they saw regression in the child's skills over a break. Think about whether your child has

difficulty retaining skills over the summer or a long break during school. If so, special education summer school is where they work on certain goals over the summer could help them not slide so much with what they remember.

As a side note, this page usually confuses everyone because it asks whether your child has difficulty with life skills and different teams interpret that in different ways. Some take it only as life skills for communication or dressing while others think any difficulty a child is having is a life skill. In my 8 years as an IEP chair, it has gone back and forth about what we are supposed to check. ***The bottom line on this page is if you feel your child would benefit from special education summer school, talk to your team about why you feel that way.**

H. Measurable Goals:

This is absolutely one of the most important sections on the IEP and can also be one of the most confusing. After seeing IEPs from different states and counties, here is what you need to know. If back on the cover and eligibility page your child has an identified area of need due to their disability, they should also have an aligned goal. So, if my child's IEP says due to their Specific Learning Disability they qualify in the areas of reading, math, behavior, and writing. I should have four separate goals. Each goal will then have between 2-4 objectives for how your child will meet that goal. They will be written to achieve within a calendar year, not a school year. This is the most important part: each goal and objective should identify how that case manager, teacher, and instructional assistant will be collecting data on that goal. It could be in the amount of targeted trials (3 out of 5), an increase in percentage (75% accuracy) or another measure. But each goal should outline these things: the overarching goal; the objectives your child will need to do to master the goal, how it will be assessed called the evaluation method (informal observation, anecdotal notes, etc.), and the frequency (so how much do they have to get to meet the goal). You will get an update on each of those goals usually with quarterly progress reports. These tend to come home with the report card.

*Because I'm honest and I want you to be prepared, make sure you understand how the school is collecting data on these goals. Sometimes the goals and objectives look really good in writing and sound good when presented at a team, but no one can show you any actual data that has been collected on how your child is achieving that goal.** I once advocated for a child with Down Syndrome who was in an inclusion setting. The team commented and were concerned about his behaviors, but no goals were aligned to that area. When reviewing this child's goals, the case manager could not share data on his specific progress

for those goals when confronted by me at the team with how they were measuring his progress.

I. Least Restrictive Environment:

This is also a very important and often strangely worded section of the IEP. This page is talking about where your child will be getting those services and what settings were considered for them to get the services. It should list how many hours they are inside the general education environment. That is the inclusion classroom where they are included with other students their age who do not have an IEP. If your child is pulled out of the classroom for an intensive reading program or for speech services, it should say on this page that they are "outside of general education." If the school is considering a self-contained placement (see the acronyms at the end of Part I), that placement will be listed on this page. Normally, those placements are not in the home school so the team will have to tell you where they are recommending these services and why. If a team is considering this type of change in placement, you should know well before this team meeting so if it is sprung on you, you have every right to ask for more information and another time when the team can meet. If other schools are offered, you should ask if you can go visit that setting and why the team thinks that is the most appropriate setting for your child.

To keep track of everything you need, I have provided you with an example of a parent checklist below.

Parent Checklist for IEP teams

_____1. I received written notice of the scheduled IEP meeting at least 10 calendar days in advance.

_____2. I was given a variety of ways I could participate in the IEP meeting (by phone, by coming into the meeting, or having the team go on without me after I gave permission).

_____3. **This is true for MD, but different states may have a different law.** I received documents for the IEP meeting 5 days in advance.

_____4. The team included appropriate staff to offer their input and make decisions regarding my child's specific needs.

_____5. Procedural safeguards (this is a large document with your rights and responsibilities) were explained to me. (This document is usually only shared once a year at an annual or for an initial request. Or if there is a disagreement.)

_____6. I provided written permission for the initial assessments. (Only at initial evaluation teams)

_____7. Assessment reports were reviewed with me. (Only at assessment review teams)

_____8. I shared information about my child and stated my expectations.

_____9. The team considered my recommendations.

_____10. The team discussed my child's participation in statewide assessments.

_____11. The IEP includes modifications and accommodations that my child needs.

_____12. The need for extended school-year services (ESY) was considered.

_____13. My child's transportation needs were considered.

_____14. I received a copy of my child's IEP and have reviewed it.

_____15. All of my questions were answered and I feel as though I understood my child's plan, especially their LRE (least restrictive environment.)

I know that is a lot of information. Believe me, it is even more overwhelming when you are looking at it surrounded by the team. That is why I wanted to give you "Look Fors" that will sum up what you need to know. Let me tell you a secret: most educators don't know all of the information on each page either. They also just go with the gist. The bottom line is that your child needs to have a plan that will help meet their needs and level the playing field for them to get the best education possible.

I wish every team had an attitude of support and willingness to work with the parent or guardian as a partner in their child's education during the TEAM process. Sadly, though I have found that is not the case. Whether it is a lack of training for educational staff members, a misunderstanding of certain disabilities or people's own biases, special education teams are not always the experts you would like them to be. I tend to get extremely passionate when I feel like a team is overlooking the best needs of a child and have advocated outside of my county for many kids. Sometimes I have advocated too passionately which has yes intimidated teams into getting things done for the child, but is not an approach I would want for you. Below are some ways on advocating respectfully. Ultimately as a parent, you just want everyone to love and see your child for his/her own unique needs. They are more than just a name on the paper and should be celebrated along with being helped by educators. Always understand that no matter how many degrees are in a room **you are the best expert on your child!**

Ways to Advocate Respectfully:

1. You know as a parent when you start to feel like perhaps the IEP or 504 plan is not being met. The child's work is not being reduced or modified. They share they are unable to take their breaks like they used to, etc. When you start to even suspect any warning signs that the IEP or 504 plan is not being met, start getting together the documents that show this. This can include assignments that have poor grades, emails or notes from the teachers, behavior reports, and any notes you take from conferences. Start gathering information.

2. Once you feel that you have concerns and some documents showing these concerns, please always schedule a teacher meeting. It is a good idea at the beginning of each school year to get your child's teachers' email addresses so you have them on hand to keep in consistent communication and/ or to schedule conferences. Come prepared to the meeting with these documents and your list of questions. Hear what the teacher has to say and get firsthand information from them. Make sure you convey an attitude and demeanor of respect towards the teacher and a willingness to want to work together with them to help support your child. Determine a way to increase communication. You can request a weekly report of your child's progress, ask them to write a note in the planner or some kind of smiley face system aligned with specific goals for your child to work on.

3. Observe your child's learning environment. I mean, aside from American Education Week. This will require being respectful of the school's visiting policy. If you'd like to come observe your child in a class, check with the teacher to see when a good date and time would be for you to come in. Frame it so they know you want to observe how your child is reacting to their learning environment in order

to get a picture of how you can best help support them with helping your child be successful.

4. If after a conference and some time, say another 4-6 weeks, you still feel that your child's needs are not being met according to their plan, put in writing a request for a team meeting (not a conference) to review their progress. Again, you will want to make sure you include the date, copy the team facilitator and the teacher along with the purpose of your request. You should get an invite for a meeting within 30 days. If you do not, send the request again in writing and this time copy the principal.

The idea is to go through the appropriate chain of command. Nothing will make a teacher more upset than skipping them with your concerns and going directly above to the principal or district office. Then you may have them intimidated but secretly they will not want to be on your side.

5. Prior to the meeting, compile all of your documents in a well-organized manner for you. I had one parent share the importance of creating and maintaining a team binder with all of the documents in one place. Write out your main concerns that you want to share at the team and the corresponding documents that show those concerns. Have your questions ready. DO NOT go into the meeting angry or hostile. Practice your tone and body language by looking in a mirror beforehand. It is hard to not get emotional in these meetings because it is your most precious gift, your child. If you do get emotional, try to convey that you just want the best help to support your child.

6. You are ready for the meeting. With your documents in hand along with your child's plan, go to the meeting with confidence. Do not be intimidated by the amount of people there. Clearly articulate your concerns, ask your questions, and hear what the team would like to put in place to address these concerns. They may want to revise the plan then or come back to another meeting. Remember, if you do not feel heard or are blown off, there are always ways within the team to document your disagreement or take your concerns to a higher level.

Final Tips for Parents:

- Be prepared to describe your child. As I shared, you are the expert on your child. Tell the team what you think your child is capable of doing now and what you see your child doing in the future.
- If you need to bring someone who knows your child. If you feel the presence of someone else an outside advocate, friend, evaluator and/or therapist's input would be helpful, tell the team leader that you are bringing them prior to the meeting so their name may be included and they can attend.

- Stay focused on your child's needs.
- Understand your options about attending the IEP meeting. If you are unable to attend in person, you can use other methods such as a phone conference, or video conference if available. Also, you and your local school system can agree to not meet for an IEP meeting and instead have a written document outlining the revisions to the IEP.

- Parent consent is required in order to start special education and related services. But after that first IEP, a parent's signature is not required for changes or later IEPs. A school system may request your signature to indicate your attendance at an IEP meeting.

Part III: Disabilities: A-Z

(with accommodations, educational implications, links to the best resources, and ways you can support your child at home)

ADD/ADHD

Definition:

Having limited strength, vitality, or alertness, including a heightened alertness to environmental stimuli, resulting in limited alertness with respect to the educational environment that is adversely affecting a student's educational performance due to health problems such as;

ADD/ADHD.

3 subtypes of ADHD:

1. **Predominantly hyperactive/impulsive type**: the individual does not show significant inattention.
2. **Predominantly inattentive type**: the individual does not show significant hyperactive-impulse behavior. It is referred to as ADD.
3. **Combined type**: The individual displays both inattentive and hyperactive-impulsive symptoms.

Characteristics of the Disability:

- Fails to give close attention to details or makes careless mistakes
- Forms letters or words poorly; messy writing
- Has difficulty sustaining attention in tasks or play activities
- Lacks follow-through on instructions and fails to finish schoolwork or chores
- Avoids or strongly dislikes tasks (such as schoolwork) that require sustained mental effort
- Is forgetful in daily activities
- Has difficulty organizing tasks and activities
- Loses things necessary for tasks or activities (pencils, assignments, tools)
- Shows difficulty engaging in leisure activities quietly
- Acts as if "driven by a motor" and cannot remain still
- Blurts out answers to questions before the questions have been completed or often interrupts others

Best accommodations for school:

- Flexible seating (the option to stand and/or alternate seating)
- Preferential seating (closest to the teacher and instruction)
- Proximity control (teacher monitoring)
- Assign tasks involving movement such as passing out papers or running errands
- Use music as a tool for transitions; song=task
- Vary tone of voice; loud, soft, whisper
- Stage assignments and divide work into smaller chunks with frequent breaks
- Teach students to verbalize a plan before solving problems or undertaking a task
- Permit a child to do something with hands while engaged in sustained listening; stress ball, worry stone, paper folding, clay, etc.
- Use inconspicuous methods such as a physical cue to signal a child when she or he appear inattentive
- Provide opportunities for students to show

divergent, creative, imaginary thinking and get peer recognition for originality
- Employ multi-sensory strategies when directions are given and lessons presented

In the area of Impulse Control:

- Ignore minor, inappropriate behavior
- Increase the immediacy of rewards/consequences
- Use time-out procedures for misbehaviors
- Supervise student closely during periods of transition
- Avoid lecturing or criticism in front of peers
- Attend to positive behavior with compliments
- Seat the student near a good role model or teacher
- Develop a behavior contract or success chart
- Call on the student only when he/she is acting appropriately
- Ignore the student when he/she is calling out
- Allow the student to be assessed orally

With Daily Organization:

- Maintain a regular structure to class assignments or procedures
- Utilize a color-coded schedule with picture graphics
- Use a color coding system to coordinate their notebook and/or book covers with schedule
- Take a photograph of desk/locker/paper organization to use a as a visual reference
- Streamline required materials
- Use peer support or cross-age tutoring

- Provide checklists for task completion
- Flag key tasks/appointments using post-its or highlighters
- Extra set/copies of assignments for home use
- Participation in academic and social skills groups

Following Directions:

- Tell the student what you expect
- Break directions down into single step directions
- Reinforce compliant behaviors
- Pose class rules in a conspicuous place (not more than five). Have students participate in developing rules.
- Provide immediate feedback
- Develop routines
- Supervise students during transitions
- Ignore minor infractions
- Reprimand in a private, appropriate manner
- Develop a clear and brief success chart (no more than 2 goals with appropriate accuracy on a daily basis)
- Involve the student in self-monitoring of his/her behavior
- Access to a recording device to record lessons, read aloud, and/or listen to prerecorded lessons or readings
- Allow the use of a computer/device to complete assignments
- List routines and mount on child's desk or notebook

What can I do at home?

1. Seek face-to-face support from family and friends-don't try to do it all alone.
2. Get up and get moving with your child.
3. Establish structure, rules, and consistent daily routines at home.
4. Learn about different strategies and resources that can help manage your child's behavior. You can try charting: sticker charts, success charts with two goals, color in charts, etc. You could also try a reward program. The important thing to remember when using charts is to understand to set the goal low at first so your child buys in. They very rarely get perfect scores on charts which is OK. They also may need a reward check in midday as opposed to waiting all day.
5. Learn how your child's diet can affect ADHD symptoms.
6. Ensure your child gets enough restful sleep.
7. Talk to your child's teachers about managing symptoms at school.
8. Learn how you can help your child make friends.
9. Learn more by reading the related articles.
10. Praise your child when they do well. Encourage and talk about their strengths more than their weaknesses.
11. Talk with your child's doctor about whether medication will help your child. A school should never tell you whether or not to give your child medicine. This is ALWAYS your decision as the parent. And as a school representative and a former parent of a child who was medicated, I understand the concerns with medications. That's why it is important to have a trusting relationship and open rapport with their pediatrician. If medication could truly help them in their mind to stay focused and feel more successful, it shouldn't be overlooked due to fear. Would we not give medicine to someone with diabetes? ADD while different can be hard to understand for a child that wants so badly to do well but can't control their own mind. Sometimes medicine is the right answer for them.
12. Monitor your child's mental health and be open to counseling. Counseling can help you and your child. It can help you deal with the challenges or raising a child with ADHD and can help your child deal with frustration, along with developing necessary self-regulation (how they deal with anger) skills as well as a healthy self-esteem.

Best resources for this disability:

- Addittudemag.org (I LOVE this resource and often refer my parents to it during team meetings.) Both my husband and I have ADD in different ways of course and it has helped me personally and professionally. If you have a Facebook account and just like their page, all the articles that pop up, you will have access to. They are extremely helpful!
- Resources to reduce fidgeting: fidget cube, fidget

spinner, rubriks cube, yoyo. Just make sure your child is using this as a fidgeting tool instead of a toy. I haven't tried the re-vibe bracelet yet but it looks promising. Also, any type of alternative seating in the classroom: bouncy chair, bands for the desk, exerciser under the desk, wobble seat, etc. Kids with the "H" in ADHD need to move to get that energy out.

Anxiety:

Definition:
A feeling of worry, nervousness, or unease, typically about an imminent event or something with an uncertain outcome. It is a general term for several disorders that cause nervousness, fear, apprehension and worrying. Here are the types of anxiety disorders:

❑ Generalized Anxiety Disorder: a chronic disorder characterized by excessive, long lasting anxiety and worry about nonspecific life events, objects, and situations.

❑ Panic Disorder: a type of anxiety characterized by brief or sudden attacks of intense terror and apprehension that leads to shaking, confusion, dizziness, nausea, and difficulty breathing. Panic attacks tend to arise abruptly and peak after 10 minutes, but they then may last for hours. Panic disorders usually occur after frightening experiences or prolonged stress, but they can also be spontaneous.

❑ Phobias: a phobia is an irrational fear and avoidance of an object or situation.

❑ Social Anxiety Disorder: is a type of social phobia characterized by a fear of being negatively judged by others or a fear of public embarrassment due to impulsive actions.

❑ Obsessive-Compulsive Disorder (OCD): is an anxiety disorder characterized by thoughts or actions that are repetitive, distressing, and intrusive. People that suffer with OCD usually know that their compulsions are unreasonable or irrational, but they serve to alleviate their anxiety. If you've ever watched Big Bang Theory, think about Sheldon knocking on Penny's door.

❑ Post-Traumatic Stress Disorder (PTSD) is anxiety that results from previous trauma. Most people only think of this term when considering someone who has been in military combat, however, this diagnosis while mostly unknown is sweeping our nation. Anyone can get PTSD at any age. This includes survivors of physical and sexual assault, abuse, accidents, disasters, and many other traumatic events. Not everyone with PTSD has been through a dangerous event. Some people get PTSD after a parent's divorce, someone they love's tragic death or even when a friend or family member experience danger or harm.

❑ Separation Anxiety Disorder is characterized by high levels of anxiety when separated from a person or place that provides feelings of security or safety. Sometimes it can result in panic.

Characteristics:

- Excessive worry most days of the week for weeks on end
- Trouble sleeping at night or sleepiness during the day
- Restlessness or fatigue during waking hours
- Trouble concentrating
- Irritability
- Constant and unreasoned fear
- Feeling of loneliness
- Sadness
- Feeling of lack of power and associated psychosomatic pains such as: headache & digestive problems

Best accommodations for school:

Anxious children tend to perform best in a calm, supportive, and organized classroom. A structured classroom that is calmly disciplined will let children feel safe and know what to expect. An ideal situation (so think about the teachers in your school parents) is a teacher who maintains authority positively, using reason and respect rather than fear or punishment. If you know a teacher like this, advocate with the administration that this is the teacher you would like your child with anxiety to have. Don't be pushy about it, just make a simple request either kindly in person or in writing. I literally at my school once had a parent get a doctor to write the name of a teacher on a prescription pad. That was way over the top too far, but I use it to make you feel better because if you know a certain teacher would not be a good match for your child with a disability speak up in a respectful way.

- Preferential seating closest to instruction and positive peer role models
(Anxious children often struggle with the unlikely fear that they will get in trouble. Seating them away from negative peer influences will be less distracting and may help them focus more.)
- Repeated directions; opportunities for them to repeat directions aloud. Non-verbal cues as needed. (Concerns about getting the directions wrong either because of a distraction or misunderstanding are common. Having a non-verbal cue with a child such as a "thumbs up" or other hand signal will let the teacher know they need their attention. Also, having directions written on the board or personalized on a post it or index card could help anxious children feel as though they understood the directions. They should also be given the opportunity to repeat the direction(s) back to the teacher.
(Class participation is another area where a non-verbal cue can be used. Fears of getting the answer wrong, saying something embarrassing or simply having other kids look at them may be concerns

for an anxious child. The teacher(s) along with you should determine your child's comfort with closed ended questions, those that require a yes or a no, or with opinion questions, start with whichever is easiest. Use a signal to let the child know that his turn is coming. Then let the child participate and answer on the topics they are the most confident.

- Extended time (time and a half or double time) on assignments and tests

(This will ease the pressure on anxious children and just knowing that the time is available may be enough for them even if they do not need to use it. Sometimes anxious children become distracted when they see other children working on their tests or turning them in and they may inaccurately assume that they don't know the material as well. Testing in an alternate, quiet location may be preferable for some children.

- Let the student know about a change in routine when possible.

(Anxious children try very hard to please and predict what is required in a situation so changes of any sort may be experienced as very stressful. When possible, like if the classroom teacher knows she is going to be absent, let the child know along with who will be the substitute. Additionally, if there is a change in time to the routine, telling them ahead of time also helps alleviate some of their stress.

- Flash pass to the guidance counselor and/or trusted adult during the school day.

Pressures can build in an anxious child's mind internally throughout the day. I've had so many teachers say they never see a child's anxiety in school and then a parent will report how they implode when they get home with all of their concerns. There is usually an internal battle we know nothing about that each anxious child has learned how to combat.

- Modified work as needed.

Anxious children can become very upset about work that they miss during an absence. Because of this, having a system in place where they can count on an assigned buddy or an extra copy of notes will help them with the make-up work. Additionally, if tests are given the day of their return, give them the option to take the test at another time.

What can I do at home?

If you suspect your child has anxiety, here is a great checklist from mendability.com that can help you recognize it. If you recognize with certainty your child has at least five of these traits, get your child some help.

✓ Pessimism and negative thinking patterns such as imagining the worst (My friends are going to hurt me; mom is going to have a car accident)
✓ Constant worry about things that might happen or have happened

- ✓ Over-exaggerating the negatives (this bad thing ALWAYS happens to me)
- ✓ Rigidity and inflexibility, self-criticism, guilty thoughts, etc. (I will never be able to do that, I will never know how to…)
- ✓ Anger
- ✓ Aggression (sometimes discreet, like quietly pushing a younger sibling, breaking someone's belonging on purpose)
- ✓ Restlessness, irritability, tantrums
- ✓ Opposition and defiance
- ✓ Crying
- ✓ Physical complaints such as stomachaches, headaches, fatigue, etc.
- ✓ Avoidance behaviors, such as avoiding things or places or refusing to do things or go places
- ✓ Sleeping difficulties, such as difficulty falling or staying asleep, nightmares or night terror
- ✓ Perfectionism (tearing off a drawing or erasing something to redo it)
- ✓ Excessive clinginess and separation anxiety (can show in acting out to force the parent to cancel an appointment to stay home)
- ✓ Procrastination (will start later, will finish in a moment)
- ✓ Poor memory and concentration
- ✓ Withdrawal from activities and family interactions
- ✓ Eating disturbances (hides to eat snacks, shows sudden aversions to some foods…)

Wow, do I wish this was available when I was a child. I would have had a lot of checks…

So if my child does have anxiety, what can I do at home?

Here are 9 ideas straight from GoZen gozen.com that parents of anxious children can try right away:

1. Stop Reassuring Your Child

Your child worries. You know there is nothing to worry about, so you say, "Trust me. There's nothing to worry about." Done and done, right? We all wish it were that simple. Why does your reassurance fall on deaf ears? It's actually not the ears causing the issue. Your anxious child desperately wants to listen to you, but the brain won't let it happen. During periods of anxiety, there is a rapid dump of chemicals and mental transitions executed in your body for survival. One by-product is that the prefrontal cortex — or more logical part of the brain — gets put on hold while the more automated emotional brain takes over. In other words, it is really hard for your child to think clearly, use logic or even remember how to complete basic tasks. What should you do instead of trying to rationalize the worry away? Try something gozen.com calls the *FEEL method*:

• **Freeze** — pause and take some deep breaths with your child. Deep breathing can help reverse the nervous system response.

- **Empathize** — anxiety is scary. Your child wants to know that you get it.
- **Evaluate** — once your child is calm, it's time to figure out possible solutions.
- **Let Go** - Let go of your guilt; you are an amazing parent giving your child the tools to manage their worry.

2. Highlight Why Worrying is Good

Remember, anxiety is tough enough without a child believing that *something is wrong with me*. Many kids even develop anxiety about having anxiety. Teach your kids that worrying does, in fact, have a purpose. When our ancestors were hunting and gathering food there was danger in the environment, and being worried helped them avoid attacks from the saber-toothed cat lurking in the bush. In modern times, we don't have a need to run from predators, but we are left with an evolutionary imprint that protects us: worry.

Worry is a protection mechanism. Worry rings an alarm in our system and helps us survive danger. Teach your kids that worry is perfectly normal, it can help protect us, and *everyone* experiences it from time to time. Sometimes our system sets off false alarms, but this type of worry (anxiety) can be put in check with some simple techniques.

3. Bring Your Child's Worry to Life

As you probably know, ignoring anxiety doesn't help. But bringing worry to life and talking about it like a real person can. Create a worry character for your child. In GoZen they created Widdle the Worrier. Widdle personifies anxiety. Widdle lives in the old brain that is responsible for protecting us when we're in danger. Of course, sometimes Widdle gets a little out of control and when that happens, we have to talk some sense into Widdle. You can use this same idea with a stuffed animal or even role-playing at home.

Personifying worry or creating a character has multiple benefits. It can help demystify this scary physical response children experience when they worry. It can reactivate the logical brain, and it's a tool your children can use on their own at any time.

4. Teach Your Child to Be a Thought Detective

Remember, worry is the brain's way of protecting us from danger. To make sure we're really paying attention, the mind often exaggerates the object of the worry (e.g., mistaking a stick for a snake). You may have heard that teaching your children to think more positively could calm their worries. But the best remedy for distorted thinking is not positive thinking; it's accurate thinking. Try a method they call the 3Cs:

- **Catch your thoughts**: Imagine every thought you have floats above your head in a bubble (like what you see in comic strips). Now, catch one of the worried thoughts like "No one at school likes me."
- **Collect evidence:** Next, collect evidence to support or negate this thought. Teach your child not to

make judgments about what to worry about based only on feelings. Feelings are not facts. (Supporting evidence: "I had a hard time finding someone to sit with at lunch yesterday." Negating evidence: "Sherry and I do homework together—she's a friend of mine.")

- **Challenge your thoughts:** The best (and most entertaining) way to do this is to teach your children to have a debate within themselves.

5. Allow Them to Worry

As you know, telling your children not to worry won't prevent them from doing so. If your children could simply shove their feelings away, they would. But allowing your children to worry openly, in limited doses, can be helpful. Create a daily ritual called "Worry Time" that lasts 10 to 15 minutes. During this ritual encourage your children to release all their worries in writing. You can make the activity fun by decorating a worry box. During worry time there are no rules on what constitutes a valid worry- anything goes. When the time is up, close the box and say good-bye to the worries for the day.

6. Help Them Go from What If to What Is

You may not know this, but humans are capable of time travel. In fact, mentally we spend a lot of time in the future. For someone experiencing anxiety, this type of mental time travel can exacerbate the worry. A typical time traveler asks what-if questions: "What if I can't open my locker and I miss class?" "What if Suzy doesn't talk to me today?"

Research shows that coming back to the present can help alleviate this tendency. One effective method of doing this is to practice mindfulness exercises. Mindfulness brings a child from what if to what is. To do this, help your child simply focus on their breath for a few minutes.

7. Avoid Avoiding Everything that Causes Anxiety

Do your children want to avoid social events, dogs, school, planes, or basically any situation that causes anxiety? As a parent, do you help them do so? Of course! This is natural. The flight part of the flight-fight-freeze response urges your children to escape the threatening situation. Unfortunately, in the long run, avoidance makes anxiety worse.

So what's the alternative? Try a method we call laddering. Kids who are able to manage their worry break it down into manageable chunks. Laddering uses this chunking concept and gradual exposure to reach a goal.

Let's say your child is afraid of sitting on the swings in the park. Instead of avoiding this activity, create mini-goals to get closer to the bigger goal (i.e., go to the edge of the park, then walk into the park, go to the swings, and, finally, get on a swing). You can use each step until the exposure becomes too easy; that's when you know it's time to move to the next rung on the ladder.

8. Help Them Work Through a Checklist

What do trained pilots do when they face an emergency? They don't wing it (no pun intended); they refer to their emergency checklists. Even with years of training, every pilot works through a checklist because, when in danger, sometimes it's hard to think clearly.

When kids face anxiety, they feel the same way. Why not create a checklist so they have a step-by-step method to calm down? What do you want them to do when they first feel anxiety coming on? If breathing helps them, then the first step is to pause and breathe. Next, they can evaluate the situation. In the end, you can create a hard copy checklist for your child to refer to when they feel anxious.

9. Practice Self-Compassion

Watching your child suffer from anxiety can be painful, frustrating, and confusing. There is not one parent who hasn't wondered at one time or another if they are the cause of their child's anxiety. Here's the thing, research shows that anxiety is often the result of multiple factors (i.e., genes, brain physiology, temperament, environmental factors, past traumatic events, etc.). Please keep in mind, you did not cause your child's anxiety, but you can help them overcome it.

Best resources for this disability:

- Addittudemag.org (This also talks about ADD/ADHD, but often there is a link between anxiety and ADD in kids)

- My book, "Benny Gator" focuses on my dog Ben who has anxiety. It is intended to be a good conversation starter for families to discuss anxiety.

- gozen.com: the list above is a good example of how gozen can help. Also check out their free youtube videos and parent resources. This year, my school purchased one of the gozen programs and it has been an invaluable resource working with kids with disabilities as it has videos and printable resources kids connect with.

Autism

Definition:

Autism is defined as a developmental disability which significantly affects verbal and non-verbal communication and social interaction, is generally noticeable before 3 years old; adversely (negatively) affects a student's educational performance and may have the following characteristics (engagement in repetitive activities and stereotyped movements, resistance to any kind of environmental change or change in daily routines, and unusual responses to sensory experiences.

Characteristics:

- communication-both verbal (spoken) and non-verbal (unspoken, such as pointing, eye contact or smiling).

- Social interactions- such as sharing emotions, understanding how others think and feel and holding a conversation, as well as the amount of time spent interacting with others
- Routines or repetitive behaviors-often called stereotyped behaviors, such as repeating words or actions, obsessively following routines or schedules, playing with toys or objects in repetitive and sometimes inappropriate ways, or having very specific and inflexible ways of arranging items

Best accommodations for school:

- Provide visual cues
- Provide visual schedules
- Pair visual schedules with frequent reminders
- Establish routines and structure in the classroom
- Familiarize students with new materials/ information prior to using them in a lesson
- Use organizers to highlight significant topics
- Reduce the number of transitions throughout the day
- Be familiar with the student's sensory needs/ preferences
- Give directions step by step, verbally, visually, and by providing physical supports and/or prompts
- Be as concrete and explicit as possible in your instructions and feedback
- Build opportunities for the student to have social and collaborative interactions throughout the regular school day

- Have consistent routines and schedules
- Prepare the student for a change by telling him/her what is going to be different and what to expect to do

What can I do at home?

- Autism is an extremely wide spectrum. Learn as much about Autism that you can.
- Know that your child is going to be who they are, and not who you want them to be. I've seen a lot of parents try to "normalize" their child with Autism. For example, a child with Autism may rather play by themselves or read a book than interact with other peers. A lot of parents have had a really hard time that their child is not interacting as much as they would like them to, however, it doesn't bother the child. Learn to recognize your own unrealistic expectations for your child. They are who they are, and have their own unique personality that should be celebrated. Never try to force them into the box of who you want them to be as opposed to who they are.
- Learn what is likely to trigger melt-downs for your child so you can do all you can to minimize them. Communicate these triggers to the school and share how you minimize melt-downs. Interact with your child and teach them the ways that are most likely to get a positive response for interacting with others.
- Children benefit from highly structured, consistent schedules and routines, especially children with Autism. They can have areas of concern such as

behavior, communication, and social skills where facilitating a structured approach to caring for your child can help greatly. There are so many resources for this these days. You can easily do an image search for a visual picture schedule and find exactly what you need. Then if you are a DIY, go to Pinterest and create exactly what you need. I'm not very decorative, so when I had my foster girls I was trying to adopt, I utilized Lakeshore learning to get responsibility charts along with visual picture schedules and Walmart to have a customizable Mason jar where we would review expectations each morning, then reward each night by placing marbles in the jar for the tasks that were achieved. There are also a lot of awesome apps, so type in Autism and see what comes up. Social skills stories are also easily found on Youtube. I like the dancing porcupines that send the message: "Don't hit, don't bite, it's wrong, not right." This has popularly resonated with kids I've shown it to.

- Assistive technology is a great tool that can be utilized for your child. Learn as much as you can about it along with how it can be offered within your child's school. This may include a simple picture communication board that helps share your child's thoughts and needs or could be more sophisticated. Either way, the team is there to help determine how this can be delivered in the school setting and normally within a school's county, there is an AT expert.

Resource:

A resource that I've found and loved is definitely nationalautismresources.com
They have different categories which describe all the products and how they can be utilized in depth. Chewelry (chewy jewelry), a sand timer, vibe mitt and tactile mat are all items I have used within my school with great success.

Another resource that truly inspired me that I've shared with teachers and parents is the story of Carly. If you just type in 20/20 interview Carly with Autism, it will pop up. This story is so inspiring. When you watch the faith this father had in his daughter in spite of what experts said about her prognosis and treatment, it will amaze you. Carly is the first child who truly expressed how she felt in her body with being non-verbal. There's also a follow up that you may have seen floating around social media as she's now a reporter who recently interviewed Channing Tatum.

*Like I've said before, as a parent, you are the expert, champion, and advocate for your child. Let this story restore your belief in that. No one truly knows the limits of any of our children with disabilities.

Developmental Delay

Definition:

This coding is commonly referred to by our public education institution through our state department but may have a different name in other states. It is used when a student from age three to age seven years old is determined to have the following: a 25% or greater delay in adaptive (social or personal behaviors), cognitive (mental as in thinking, reasoning or remembering), communicative (talking and/or willingness to talk to people), emotional (relating to emotions), physical (fine and gross motor skills), or social (the gaining of skills, relationships and attitudes that enable one to interact with society) development. If a child has atypical (unusual) development or behavior and/or a diagnosed physical or mental condition within that age group they can also be coded under this type of disability categorization.

Characteristics of the disability:

- Difficulty interacting with others and developing relationships with peers, educators and authority figures and family
- Has trouble understanding social rules
- Focuses on objects for long periods of time and may enjoy this more than other activities
- May not seek love and approval from a teacher or parent
- May become unusually frustrated when trying to do simple tasks (that most children of the same age can do)
- Rarely makes eye contact
- May not appear to notice others and seems to tune people out
- Often does not build relationships with others their age at a developmental level expected
- Rarely shares attention with others, such as by showing something, pointing, or pointing out interests or accomplishments
- Does not demonstrate emotional reciprocity (taking turns)
- Rarely imitates the actions of others in play or otherwise
- Does not know how to play with supplies, equipment and materials the way they are intended
- Seems to be in his/her "own world"
- Is not interested in other children

Best accommodations in the classroom:

In the area of Physical Development:

- Plan physical activities for times when the student has the most energy
- Provide simple, fun obstacle courses that the student is capable of completing
- Provide daily opportunities and activities for children to use handheld tools and objects
- Use songs with finger plays to develop fine motor skills

- Use materials such as a non-slip mat under drawing paper, thick crayons, and thick handled paint brushes that are easy to grasp
- Incorporate singing and dancing into many activities
- Place objects in student's hand to hold and feel
- Let students practice swinging and hitting
- When eating, let the student make a mess to practice the motions of feeding and cleaning up
- Give students blocks, clay, paper, pencils, crayons, safety scissors, play dough, and manipulatives to use
- Plan daily physical activities, and take students outside to run, climb, and jump around
- Have students practice buttoning and unbuttoning, zipping clothes, and opening and closing a door
- Use activities that involve cutting, pasting, drawing, and writing
- Model and use activities with drawing and writing tools
- Use child-size tables and chairs in the classroom
- Have a schedule for active and quiet times
- Model and talk about healthy eating habits with students
- Provide nutritious snacks and meals
- Make parents aware of health concerns that could affect a child's development (changes in growth, hearing, vision)
- Provide parents with information about health, medical, and dental resources
- Use visual discrimination games such as "I spy"

- Take "listening walks"

Cognitive Development:

- Acknowledge level of achievement by being specific
- Allow student time to complete tasks and practice skills at their own pace
- Use the student's preferences and interests to build lessons
- Be specific when giving praise and feedback
- Break down tasks into smaller steps
- Demonstrate steps, and then have student repeat the steps, one at a time
- Be as concrete as possible
- Demonstrate what you mean rather than giving directions verbally
- Show a picture when presenting new information verbally
- Provide hands-on materials and experiences
- Share information about how things work
- Pair student with a buddy who can assist with keeping the student on track
- Be consistent with classroom routines
- Set a routine so the student knows what to expect
- Provide a visual schedule of activities that can be understood by the student (using photos, icons
- Use a visual timer so student knows when an activity will be over and they can transition to the next task
- Use age appropriate materials
- Use short and simple sentences to ensure understanding

- Repeat instructions or directions frequently
- Ask the student if further clarification is necessary
- Keep distractions and transitions to a minimum
- Teach specific skills whenever necessary
- Provide an encouraging and supportive learning environment
- Do not overwhelm a student with multiple or complex instructions
- Speak more slowly and leave pauses for student to process your words
- Speak directly to the student
- Speak in clear short sentences
- Ask one question at a time and provide adequate time for student to reply

Communication Development:

- Use large clear pictures to reinforce what you are saying
- Speak slowly and deliberately
- Paraphrase back what the student has said
- Clarify types of communication methods the student may use
- Identify and establish functional communication systems for students who are non-verbal
- Reinforce communication attempts (e.g. their gestures, partial verbalizations) when the student is non-verbal or emerging verbal
- Label areas in the room with words and pictures
- Use sequencing cards to teach order of events
- Provide puppets/pictures as props when using finger plays and songs
- Develop a procedure for the student to ask for help
- Speak directly to the student
- Be a good speech model
- Have easy and good interactive communication in classroom
- Consult a speech language pathologist concerning your class
- Be aware that students may require another form of communication
- Encourage participation in classroom activities and discussions
- Provide assistance and positive reinforcement as the student shows the ability to do something with increased independence
- Use gestures that support understanding
- Model correct speech patterns
- Be patient when the student is speaking, since rushing may result in frustration
- Focus on interactive communication
- Use active listening
- Incorporates the student's interests into speech.
- Use storybook sharing in which a story is read to student and responses are elicited (praise is given for appropriate comments about the content)

Social and Emotional Development:

- Use strategies to assist the student in separating from the parent
- Set a routine in saying goodbye (such as finding a

book to read)
- Value and acknowledge the student's efforts
- Provide opportunities for students to play in proximity to one another
- Provide opportunities for students to interact directly with each other
- Work to expand the child's repertoire of socially mediated reinforcers (e.g. tickling, peek-a-boo, chase, etc.).
- Explore feelings through the use of play
- Teach students to express their feelings in age-appropriate ways
- Provide play activities that don't require sharing such as art projects, making music (students have their own instrument), and sand or water play
- Ask students to imagine how their behavior might affect others
- Have students make a "friend book" with students from the class
- When dealing with conflict, explain what happened in as few words as possible and use a calm, not-angry voice
- Point out natural consequences of the student's behavior
- Brainstorm better choice(s) with students
- Use language to describe feelings and experiences
- Put student's feelings into words
- Read books about feelings
- Explain your reasons for limits and rules in language that students can understand

- Model the benefits involved in cooperating
- Use natural consequences when possible to reinforce cause and effect involved in a rule, request, or limit
- Teach the students words for important people and things

Adaptive Behavior (everyday skills for functioning):
- Explicitly teach life skills related to daily living and self-care
- Break down each skill into steps
- Use visual schedules with pictures and icons to demonstrate each step
- Plan experiences that are relevant to the child's world
- Find ways to apply skills to other settings (field trips)
- Minimize distractions and the possibility for over-stimulation
- Teach and model personal hygiene habits such as washing hands, covering mouth and nose when sneezing or coughing, and dental care
- Find ways to practice personal care and self-help skills (using centers in the classroom)
- Provide opportunities for students to practice asking for help, feeding themselves, dressing, washing hands, toileting, and locating personal items
- Provide materials that support self-care such as a child-size sink, toilet, coat rack, and toothbrushes
- Teach and model rules and practices for bus safety, playground safety, staying with the group, and

safety in the classroom

- Teach students to provide personal identification information when asked
- Teach and model procedures for dealing with potentially dangerous situations, including fire, severe weather, and strangers

How can I help at home?

- Learn the signs and act early. Talk with your child's doctor right away if you have any concerns with their developmental milestones.
- Write down observations you notice about your child's progress. Include dates and keep this as a log over time to refer to when talking with their doctor.
- Do not base their developmental milestones off of their siblings. Also consider other contributing factors such as whether they were premature or not.
- Seek early intervention within the county's school system as we talked about in part II.
- Connect with other parents whose children have developmental delays.
- Be patient with the process.
- Get siblings (if they have them) involved so they do not feel left out.
- Work together through play opportunities.

Best resources for this disability:

http://www.parentcenterhub.org/repository/dd/
http://www.firstsigns.org/
understood.org

mychildwithoutlimits.org

Emotional Disability

Definition:

This is not a code that should be taken lightly or given out by an educational institution without a variety of assessment tools. It is a condition where a child shows one or more of the following things over a long period of time and to a very high degree that greatly and negatively impacts their performance in the classroom. A student with this coding has one or more of the following: an inability to learn that cannot be explained by an intellectual, sensory or any health factor(s), an inability to build or keep good interpersonal relationships with peers and teachers, inappropriate types of behavior or feelings under normal circumstances, a general, pervasive mood of unhappiness or depression or a tendency to show physical symptoms or fears associated with personal or school problems.

Characteristics of the Disability:

- An inability to learn that cannot be explained by intellectual, sensory, or health factors
- An inability to build or maintain satisfactory interpersonal relationships with peers and teachers
- Inappropriate types of behavior or feelings under normal circumstances

- A general pervasive mood of unhappiness or depression
- A tendency to develop physical symptoms or fears associated with personal or school problems
- Hyperactivity (short attention span, impulsiveness)
- Aggression or self-injurious behavior (acting out, fighting)
- Withdrawal (not interacting socially with others, excessive fear or anxiety)
- Immaturity (inappropriate crying, temper tantrums, poor coping skills)
- Learning difficulties (academically performing below grade level)

Some disorders that fall into this category are:

Conduct Disorders:

Children with conduct disorder act inappropriately, infringe on the rights of others and violate the behavioral expectations of other. CD is defined as a repetitive behavioral pattern of violating the rights of others or societal norms. Three of the following criteria, or symptoms listed below are required over a 12 month period for a diagnosis of CD and one of the three criteria must have occurred in the past 6 months.
- bullies, threatens, or intimidates others
- picks fights
- has used a dangerous weapon
- has been physically cruel to people
- has been physically cruel to animals
- has stolen while confronting a victim (for example,

mugging or extortion)
- has forced someone into sexual activity
- has deliberately set a fire with the intention of causing damage
- has deliberately destroyed property of others
- has broken into someone else's house or car
- frequently lies to get something or to avoid obligations
- has stolen without confronting a victim or breaking and entering (e.g., shoplifting or forgery)
- stays out at night; breaks curfew (beginning before 13 years of age)
- has run away from home overnight at least twice (or once for a lengthy period)
- is often truant from school (beginning before 13 years of age)

Oppositional Defiant Disorders:

Less serious, and less aggressive than a conduct disorder, children with oppositional defiance disorder still tend to be negative, argumentative and defiant. Children with oppositional defiance are not aggressive, violent or destructive, as are children with conduct disorder, but their inability to cooperative with adults or peers often isolates them and creates serious impediments to social and academic success.

Psychiatric Disorders:

This can include bipolar (manic depression) disorder, schizophrenia, anxiety disorder (can also fall under

Other Health Impairment), eating disorders and psychotic disorders.

Best accommodations for school:

- Provide positive behavior supports
- Be familiar with the student's Functional Behavior Assessment (FBA) and Behavior Intervention Plan (BIP)
- Provide a consistent and structured behavior approach for addressing behavior
- Provide social skills instruction. This can occur through a small group setting as well as through a social story targeted on the specific behaviors your child is demonstrating that they have to read and review throughout the school day.

School staff will also need to accept some general philosophical ideas about students and behaviors. This is especially important to this disability coding:

1. Students don't generally act badly because they want to be bad. Rather, they act out when they cannot figure out how to express themselves, when they are struggling with how to predict their environment, when they are not sure what else to do, or when they don't know how to respond to a situation to or initiate an interaction.
2. Students with an emotional disability may truly not comprehend a teacher's directions, the subject they are studying, or the social milieu of the classroom. It may have nothing to do with a teacher's ability to

teach, and everything to do with what is happening inside the mind of that student.

What can I do at home?

Listen to what others are telling you about your child and act as their strongest advocate. Keep in mind that even though certain aspects of school or social interactions may have been easy for you growing up, your child may have different needs and strengths than you did.

It is unrealistic to believe that one teacher with thirty students is going to be able to spend a significant amount of time with every child in a single class period. Start asking for help if others remark that your child seems depressed, out of control, or hyperactive. Don't take these comments personally, but rather use this information to ask questions in order to assist her. If she continues to struggle, request a complete evaluation to determine if she needs additional support. Don't be too proud to accept help!

Also, parents can struggle with reaching out to hospitals and mental health institutions. I know how hard it is to even consider making this call to have to have your child evaluated at a mental health institution. However, if they are displaying behaviors that are harmful to themselves or others and you are out of your realm in handling them, the best thing to do can be to get professional outside assistance.

Best resources for this disability:

http://www.parentcenterhub.org/repository/

emotionaldisturbance/
http://www.pacer.org/cmh/
http://elementaryemotionaldisturbance.weebly.com/
for-parents.html
https://www.naset.org/emotionaldisturbance2.0.html
https://www.nami.org/#

Intellectual Disability

Definition:

This disability used to be named under the coding of mental retardation. Intellectual Disability is the most up to date coding for a student who has general intellectual functioning affecting a student's educational performance which is significantly below average, exists concurrently with adaptive behavior; and is manifested during the developmental period. I just listed three specific traits of this disability and unlike the category before it where there was an "or" for each characteristic, under this category the student must meet them ALL for this to be the right category.

Basic Criteria of this coding:

• Significantly sub-average general intellectual functioning (IQ of 70 or below)
• Significant challenges in adapting to living and work environments

This is a very broad category that includes a wide range of skills, and needs all that may need support.

Learning Characteristics:

• Slow rate of learning
• Thinks in a concrete way
• Difficulties generalizing (cannot take knowledge learned in one situation and apply it to another)
• Needs to be taught how to make choices (difficulty applying past experiences to current decision making)
• Challenges in setting goals and problem solving (needs steps broken down into smaller steps. Needs help to figure out problems and steps to reach them)
• Memory problems (has difficulty with tasks that take several steps or that are not in their routine. Training needs to be included with lots of opportunities for practice, feedback and repetition),
• Short attention span (cannot stick with an activity or focus their attention for long periods of time)
• Expressive language (difficulty sharing ideas and feelings to other people, identifying they don't understand something and/or asking questions)

Best accommodations for school:

• Use concrete items and examples to explain new concepts and provide practice in existing skill areas
• Model desired behaviors, and clearly identify what behaviors you expect in the classroom
• Use appropriate communication methods such as Makaton signing for pre verbal students or those with beginning language. Makaton is a language program that uses signs and symbols to help people to communicate. It is designed to support spoken

language and the signs and symbols are used with speech, in spoken word order. With Makaton, children and adults can communicate straight away using signs and symbols. Many people then drop the signs or symbols naturally at their own pace, as they develop speech. Find out more at: https://www.makaton.org/aboutMakaton/

- Do not overwhelm a student with multiple or complex instructions.
- Use strategies such as chunking, backward shaping and role modeling as helpful teaching approaches
- Be explicit (verbal, visual & written) about what it is you want a student to do
- Learn about the needs and characteristics of your student, but do not automatically assume they will behave the same way today as they did yesterday
- Ask for their input about how they feel they learn best, and help them to be as in control of their learning as possible
- Put skills in context so there is a reason for learning tasks
- Involve families and significant others in learning activities, planning and special days, as well as in informing you about the needs of their young person

What can I do at home?

- Learn as much as you can about intellectual disability
- Help your child to become independent and foster responsibility with daily life skills such as dressing, feeding themselves, using the bathroom, and grooming
- Assign your child chores. Keep their age, abilities, and attention span in mind. Then model how to do those chores and/or have a visual reminder of how to complete those shores along with breaking them down into smaller steps. Help them when they need assistance and give them ongoing feedback about the chores. Praise your child when they do the chores well to build their confidence.
- When possible, use real-world examples to help reinforce what your child is learning at school. If they are learning how to count money, give them the opportunity to count the coins when you go to the grocery store together.
- Search within your community for extracurricular or social opportunities such as scouts, recreation center activities, church picnics, sports, and so on that will give your child the opportunities to socially interact with others which will help them build social skills.
- Meet with your child's educational team of teachers to find out how you can support your child's learning at home.

Specific Learning Disability

Definition:

A disorder in one or more of the basic psychological processes involved in understanding or in using language, spoken or written, that may manifest itself in the imperfect ability to listen, think, speak, read, write, spell or do mathematical calculations. It includes conditions such as perceptual disabilities, brain injury, minimal brain dysfunction, dyslexia and developmental aphasia.

It **does not** include students who have learning problems primarily in the result of:
- visual
- hearing
- motor impairment
- intellectual disability
- emotional disturbance
- environmental
- cultural or economic disadvantage

Characteristics of the disability:

- Short attention span
- Poor memory
- Difficulty following directions
- Inability to discriminate between/among letters, numerals, or sounds
- Poor reading and/or writing ability
- Eye-hand coordination problems; poorly coordinated
- Difficulties with sequencing
- Disorganization and other sensory difficulties
- Performs differently from day to day
- Responds inappropriately in many instances

- Distractible, restless, impulsive
- Says one thing but means another
- Doesn't adjust well to change
- Difficulty listening and remembering
- Difficulty telling time and knowing right from left
- Difficulty sounding out words
- Reverses letters
- Places letters in incorrect sequence
- Delayed speech development; immature speech

Best accommodations for school:

- Increase the amount of modeling, demonstration, and guided practice
- Develop routines for repetitive activities. This will help students to successfully follow through on activities.
- Seat the student near a well-focused study buddy to provide peer assistance in note taking and checking work
- Use a study carrel or privacy board for seat work
- Teach the student to use visualization and association method to create mental hooks to retrieve information (Pictionary)
- Break longer assignments into smaller components
- Pair written and oral instructions with a picture example (mental hook) to help the student retrieve information from long-term memory
- End of day check by teacher/aide for expected books/materials to take home for homework
- Allow extra time for student to retrieve information

to complete tasks
- Shorten assignments or work periods to coincide with the student's attention span
- Many opportunities for hands-on projects to assist in concept retention
- Design classwork assignments so that the student has repetition of new material in a variety of forms

In Reading:
- Provide extra time for completion, shortened assignments, simplified text, chapter outlines
- Reduce the number of students in an instructional group
- Highlight key concepts
- Utilize story frames, before, during and after strategies, echo reading, story mapping; VAKT (visual, auditory, kinesthetic and tactile) learning approaches, graphic organizers, structured study guides, KWL charts, peer support, cross-age training

In Math:
- Reduce the number of students in an instructional group
- Reduce the number of problems
- Eliminate the need to copy problems
- Enlarge worksheet for increased space
- Avoid mixing operational signs on the page/row
- Provide extended/adjusted time for completing
- Use procedural checklists

- Highlight operational signs
- Use graph paper for set up
- Used raised number lines
- Incorporate "real-life" tasks
- Utilize mnemonic devices
- Use color coding strategies
- Use peer support or cross-age tutoring
- Include VAKT (visual, auditory, kinesthetic and tactile) opportunities

With Written Expression:
- Reduce the number of students in an instructional group
- Provide extended/adjusted time for completion
- Modified assignments
- Use a study carrel for reduced distractions
- Provide graphic organizers with sentence starters
- Provide story frames
- Utilize oral compositions with a scribe
- Use oral proofreading to check for meaning and clarity
- Utilize mnemonic devices
- Include VAKT opportunities
- Use color coding strategies
- Utilize a recording device for oral pre-writing, composition, and/or editing.
- Provide access to a laptop or other device with an electronic dictionary/thesaurus.
- If applicable and available, provide access to assistive technology.

Modifying the instructional setting:

- Move a student to another area of the room
- Limit the student's engagement with others
- Modifying the course presentation:
- Put fewer problems on the page
- Give both verbal and written instructions (or instructions through pictures)
- Have one student read with another who is struggling
- Allow oral responses in place of written ones
- Provide modifications to textbooks
- Allow the student to pick between two academic options
- Modifying course expectations:
- Change the grading rubric
- Accept partially completed assignments
- Negotiate with a struggling student regarding the number of problems she thinks she can complete during a class period- then stick to that agreement
- Allow the student additional time to complete her assignment (without taking away recess or lunch)

What can I do at home?

- Learn about the different type of learning disabilities as the more you know the more you can help your child.
- Offer praise to your child as often as you can. It is important to realize that kids with learning disabilities are often trying the best that they can and they have different areas of strengths often that are not associated with academics. Pursue extracurricular activities in your child's area of interest (dance, art, sports, etc.) so they can feel successful.
- Determine your child's learning style. This is normally visual (looking), tactile (touching materials through hands on practice), auditory (listening) or kinesthetic (through movement).
- Make homework a priority and set a homework routine that can help your child be confident and successful. Homework should not be taking hours. If homework causes stress and anxiety for you and your child to get it completed, reach out to the teacher to get some guidance on how homework can be reduced or modified. Usually the amount of homework a child should have should be ten minute increments based on the grade (grade 1=10 minutes; grade 2=20; grade 3=30; grade 4=40, grade 5=50, etc.)
- Monitor your child's mental health as well as your own. Don't be discouraged at considering counseling or other resources that can help your child deal with frustration, build confidence and healthy self-esteem. Having a learning disability is tough. Those that have one watch other students the same age who do not struggle as much and may put in a lot less effort. It can really make them feel as though something is wrong with them which over time, really affects one's self esteem.
- Build a network and talk with other parents of children who have learning disabilities. Call

NICHCY (18006950285) and ask how to find parent groups near you. They can also put you in touch with the parent training and information center in your state.

- Be an advocate for your child by meeting with school personnel through conferences or teams any time you feel that your child's plan needs updated with specific accommodations.
- Make sure you establish, maintain and continue to facilitate a positive working relationship with your child's teacher. It is important that they feel you are a partner with them in helping your child succeed.

Speech Language Impairment:

Definition:
A communication disorder such as stuttering, impaired articulation, a language impairment, or a voice impairment that negatively affects a child's educational performance.

Characteristics:

Signs of a speech sound disorder:
- Says p, b, m, h and w incorrectly in words (1-2 years old)
- Says k, g, f, t, d, and n incorrectly in words (2-3 years old)
- Produces speech that is unclear, even to familiar people (2-3 years old)

Signs of stuttering:
- Struggles to say sounds or words (2 ½-3 years old)
- Repeats first sounds of words- "b-b-b-ball" for "ball" (2 ½ -3 years old)
- Pauses a lot while talking (2 ½-3 years old)
- Stretches sounds out- "f-f-f-f-farm" for "farm" (2 ½-3 years old)

Signs of a language disorder:
- Does not smile or interact with others (birth and older)
- Does not babble (4-7 months old)
- Makes only a few sounds or gestures, like pointing (7-12 months old)
- Does not understand what others say (7 months-2 years old)
- Says only a few words (12-18 months old)
- Words are not easily understood (18 months-2 years old)
- Does not put words together to make sentences (1 ½-3 years old)
- Has trouble playing and talking with other children (2-3 years old)
- Has trouble with early reading and writing skills (2 ½-3 years old)

Signs of a voice disorder:
- Uses a hoarse or breathy voice
- Uses a nasal sounding voice

Best accommodations for school:

For Language:
- Focus on interactive communication
- Use active listening
- Incorporate the student's interests into speech
- Ensure that the student has a way to appropriately express their wants and needs
- Reinforce communication attempts (i.e., their gestures, partial verbalizations) when the student is non-verbal or emerging verbal
- Paraphrase back what the student has said or indicated
- Use storybook sharing in which a story is read to student and responses are elicited (praise is given for appropriate comments about the content).
- Ask open-ended appropriate questions
- Use linguistic scaffolding techniques that involve a series of questions
- Use language for social interaction and to resolve conflicts
- Emphasize goals and tasks that are easy for the student to accomplish
- Work at the student's pace
- Present only one concept at a time
- Have the speech therapist present language units to the entire class
- Use computers in the classroom for language enhancement
- Encourage reading and writing daily
- Use tactile and visual cues (e.g., pictures, 3-D objects)
- Incorporate vocabulary with unit being taught
- Provide fun activities that are functional and practical

For Speech (Articulation):
- Develop a procedure for the student to ask for help
- Speak directly to the student
- Be a good speech model
- Have easy and good interactive communication in classroom
- Consult a speech language pathologist concerning your assignments and activities
- Encourage participation in classroom activities and discussions
- Model acceptance and understanding in classroom
- Anticipate areas of difficulty and involve the student in problem-solving
- Provide assistance and provide positive reinforcement when the student shows the ability to do something unaided
- Use a peer-buddy system when appropriate
- Devise alternate procedures for an activity with students
- Use gestures that support understanding
- Model correct speech patterns and avoid correcting speech difficulties

Additional Accommodations for the Classroom:

- Reduce unnecessary classroom noise as much as possible
- Be near the student when giving instructions and ask the student to repeat the instructions and prompt when necessary
- Provide verbal clues often
- Provide a quiet spot for the student to work if possible
- Speak clearly and deliberately
- Provide visual cues- on the board or chart paper
- Redirect the student frequently and provide step by step directions- repeating when necessary
- Allow students to tape lectures
- Allow more time for the student to complete activities
- Modify classroom activities so they may be less difficult, but have the same learning objectives
- Allow more time for the student to complete assignments and tests
- Design tests and presentations that are appropriate for the student (written instead of oral)
- Divide academic goals into small units, utilizing the same theme
- Provide social and tangible rewards to reinforce desired behaviors
- Focus on the student's strengths as much as possible
- Have the student sit in an accessible location to frequently monitor their understanding
- Allow extra time to complete work because of distractions, slow handwriting, or problems in decoding text
- Have routines that students can follow
- Use a visual reminder of the day's events to help with organization
- Establish communication goals related to student work experiences and plan strategies for the transition from school to employment and adult life
- Be patient when the student is speaking, since rushing may result in frustration
- Be aware of the student's functioning level in auditory skills, semantics, word recall, syntax, phonology, and pragmatics (and how they affect academic performance)

What can I do at home?

For a speech sound disorder:
- Say the sounds correctly when you talk; it's okay if you make some mistakes with sounds
- Do not correct speech sounds as it is more important that you keep your child talking

For stuttering:
- Do not rush your child when they are talking; give them time to talk and get out what they want to say
- Don't interrupt or stop your child when they're speaking
- See an SLP if you are concerned (often young children may suffer from stuttering for a short time and then it will stop)

For a language disorder:

- Talk with the child in the language you are most comfortable using
- Talk, read, and play with your child along with listening and responding to your child
- Talk about what you are doing and what your child is doing
- Use a lot of different words with your child
- Use longer sentences as your child gets older
- Have your child play with other children

For a voice disorder:

- See a doctor if your child sounds breathy, hoarse, or has a nasally sounding voice
- Tell your child not to scream or shout
- Keep your child away from cigarette smoke

Best resources:

identifythesigns.org

www.mommyspeechtherapy.com

Traumatic Brain Injury:

Definition:

Traumatic brain injury (TBI), also called acquired brain injury or simply head injury, occurs when a sudden trauma causes damage to the brain. TBI can result when the head suddenly and violently hits an object, or when an object pierces the skull and enters brain tissue.

Characteristics:

Traumatic Brain Injury is a condition caused by a head injury that results in lasting damage to the brain. This injury disrupts normal brain functioning and may permanently impact how a person acts, moves, and/or thinks.

Traumatic brain injury is one of the categories of disability specified in IDEA. This means that a child with traumatic brain injury may be eligible for special education and related services if it adversely affects their education.

A traumatic brain injury often impacts functioning in the following areas:

Memory and cognition, social skills, emotional regulation, attention, behavior, speech and language, and physical health.

Memory and Cognition:

- Difficulty with logic, problem solving, and reasoning
- Slower to respond, react and complete activities and tasks
- Difficulty remembering facts, procedures, events, etc.
- Frequently struggles with grade level work
- Difficulty storing new information, working memory deficits
- Difficulty retrieving old information
- May be disoriented with time, places, and people
- Difficulty sequencing events
- Physical and verbal perseverations (repeating a word, phrase, or action, over and over again)

Social Skills and Emotional Regulation

- Inappropriate social behaviors
- Emotional responses may be unpredictable in nature and severity
- Difficulty regulating emotions
- May struggle to accurately interpret verbal and non-verbal cues
- Emotional responses may not "fit" the situation
- Emotional instability (happy one moment, sad the next)

Inattention and Impulsivity

- Difficulty focusing attention
- May have difficulty controlling impulses, thoughts, and feelings
- Injury and memory loss may impact successful use of behavior modification strategies
- Distracted by internal and external events and thoughts

Speech and Language

- May have speech and language deficits (should be checked frequently)
- Difficulty speaking words or phrases
- Difficulty comprehending what others say
- May struggle to follow multi-step instructions

Physical

- May struggle to process visual information (visual perceptual issues)
- May experience visual deficits such as double vision and partial loss of vision
- May have visual "blind spots"
- Possible coma could produce some slowing and lethargy
- Seizures are common following a head injury, and seizure medication may cause "cognitive dulling"
- Difficulty staying awake
- Inability to recognize post-injury deficits
- Possible gross or fine motor deficits depending on what part of the brain was injured (may have some paralysis)
- Short periods of disorientation or attention lapse
- May tire frequently and quickly

Symptoms of TBI can range from mild to severe (see below for what this can look like at each level)

Mild TBI:

- Fatigue
- Headaches
- Visual disturbances
- Memory loss
- Poor attention/concentration
- Sleep disturbances
- Dizziness/loss of balance
- Irritability/emotional disturbances
- Feelings of depression
- Seizures
- Possible coma
- Nausea

- Loss of smell
- Sensitivity to light and sounds
- Mood changes
- Getting lost or confused
- Slowness in thinking
- Moderate TBI:
- Results in permanent brain damage
- Produces lifelong deficits (to varying degrees)
- Death may occur
- Seizures
- Coma (to varying degrees)
- Confusion
- Difficulty with "thinking skills" (memory, attention, judgment)
- Blurred vision, loss of vision
- Change in hearing acuity
- Ringing in ears
- Slurred speech
- Difficulty understanding spoken language
- Difficulty processing sensory input (touch, smell, hearing, etc.)
- Personality changes
- Loss of taste and/or smell
- Paralysis
- Lethargy
- Loss of bowel/bladder control
- Dizziness
- Inappropriate emotional responses
- Severe TBI:
- Results in significant permanent brain damage

- May result in total loss of speech ability
- Produces lifelong deficits to a severe degree
- May require lifetime care and assistance
- Sustained loss of consciousness
- Can result in death
- May exhibit signs of poor self-concept, depression, isolation, withdrawal, and paranoia
- Poor judgment and reasoning skills

Best accommodations for school:

- Extended time (time and a half) or (double time) to complete assignments in class
- Multiple or frequent breaks
- A copy of lesson notes and or the powerpoint presentation of the lesson
- Audio recording of lessons for students to playback later
- Pair verbal with written directions; repeat directions as needed along with having students repeat directions
- Allow the use of a computer or device that has spell check and grammar checks; model with the student how to use this prior to ongoing, daily use
- When grading work, reduce the emphasis on spelling and grammatical errors unless it is the purpose of the assignment
- Permit the use of a dictionary or thesaurus for assignments; again model with the student how to use this prior to ongoing use

- Preferential seating closest to instruction and the teacher
- Modify quantity of work by length but not complexity (ex. if there are 5 of the same skill set of questions, only have the child do 3)
- Avoid placing the student in high pressure academic situations (competitions)
- Exempt the student from reading aloud in front of their classmates because of impaired reading skills
- Chunking of assignments
- Scribing for students (writing and/or typing what they say) as needed
- Use of calculation devices on assignments and tests

What can I do at home?

- Ask questions and work with your child's medical team to understand your child's injury and treatment plan. Remember, you are an important partner with them and will be monitoring the implementation of this plan so be sure to ask questions and make recommendations to them.
- Maintain all important medical documents and information in regards to your child's treatment. It is important to log this information in whatever type of organizational system you want to use (binder, folder, scanning in to a digital folder, etc.). As you meet with doctors, nurses and others, write down what they say. Put in your system any paperwork you receive. If the school or anyone else working with your child needs this information, always ask

them to make a copy as opposed to giving them the original.
- Consult with the personnel at your child's school to see the best next steps. If your child was in that school prior to the injury work with them to develop an appropriate plan for their return along with an IEP as needed. Share the medical information with that team or invite medical personnel to share that information.
- Maintain ongoing communication with your child's teacher in order to determine how they are doing in school. Make sure she understands the effects your child's TBI can have on their learning (day to day they may not remember skills).

Last but not least, let's touch on a category that a lot of educational systems are falling flat in meeting the student's needs in:

Twice Exceptional

Definition:
Twice exceptional which is often shortened to 2e refers to intellectually gifted children who have some form of disability. These children are considered exceptional both because of their intellectual gifts and because of their special needs. There is no clear-cut profile of twice exceptional children because the nature and causes of twice exceptionality are so varied.

Characteristics of twice-exceptional children: (they may show one or all of the following)

- discrepancy between verbal and written work
- creativity
- excellence on tasks requiring abstract concepts
- difficulty with tasks requiring memorization
- anxiety
- depression
- acting out behavior
- poor organization
- poor motivation
- active problem solving
- analytic thinking
- strong task commitment when interested
- withdrawal/shyness

Best accommodations for school:

- Allow students to explore their interests by providing choices within the learning activities
- Vary the teaching style to involve more visual and kinesthetic (hands on) formats
- Praise and provide opportunities for those students to shine
- Teach concepts before teaching content. Twice exceptional students may show difficulty memorizing details bur are good at grasping the big picture. An example may include showing the student a video trailer of a book prior to having them read the novel.
- Use compacting to accommodate their gifts as allowed within the county's guidelines. Compacting refers to allowing students to demonstrate their mastery of the curriculum before the unit begins. So give them the assessment first to see what they already know and then just fill in the gaps instead of having them participate in each portion of the entire unit.
- Implement complexity in lessons while also scaffolding the teaching. What often happens to our gifted students in education is that they are just required to do more of something. But with twice exceptional students, they may get overwhelmed. Chunking their assignments or limiting the amount of problems showing the same skill they have to complete are ways to support them.
- Providing students with organizational skills such as a calendar, planner, graphic organizers and reduced distractions within their learning environment.

What can I do at home?

- Create a safe home environment
- Nurture strengths and interests
- Foster a "Yes, I Can" Attitude
- Support the Development of Compensatory Strategies (Ways they cope and make up for their gaps due to their disability)
- Promote Positive Coping Strategies
- Cultivate Resiliency
- Coach Realistic Goal Setting

- Encourage Children to Become Independent Learners
- Advocate for your child respectfully

Best resources for 2e parents:
- 2elearners.org
- 2enewsletter.com

Conclusion

I know that was a lot of information. I encourage you to continue to use this book as a reference guide for whatever information you need to come back and refer to as often as you need to come back to it. You may only be able to handle one portion at a time. Please know if you need further assistance with an educational situation with your child and would like more customized advice, I invite you to send me a message sharing your story: www.kingkahan.com

The roadmap to navigating a child's disability is one of the hardest challenges in life because there is not a clearly paved descriptive path that works consistently for every single child. And often you move sideways and/or backwards before you ever feel like your child is consistently progressing forward. The most important things to remember are to embrace who your child is no matter what their needs are, to continue to be their biggest cheerleader, advocate and coach and most importantly to remember what an awesome parent you are. You will make mistakes, you will want to give up, and you will feel as though your child is taking one step forward and ten steps back. Other people without kids with disabilities will never truly understand all that you go through and sometimes will pity you never realizing the special blessing it is to truly love and be loved by a child with a disability. And most of the time you will feel depleted in your endless persistence with trying to educate the world on having an understanding of your child's needs so they can look at them with compassion instead of a mentality of "what's wrong with them." And because I know you don't hear it enough: Thank you for all you do as a parent! You are enough and you've got this!

There is a good visual out there that says: "It takes a special kind of person to care for a child with special needs." This sentence is then crossed out and replaced with: "A child with special needs will inspire you to be a special kind of person." Each child that I have encountered with special needs has changed my life, outlook and perspective in so many ways. They have enabled me to be not only the best educator I can, but a better human being and I am so thankful to continue to learn from them.

A lot of society has a misconception that students with special needs, especially those involving behavioral supports in the form of positive reinforcement get rewards unfairly. Something I have heard a lot as an assistant principal is "What about the other kids? What do they get? It isn't fair for them." It took a long time for me to truly know how to respond to this question to help people "get it." Thankfully at one class I attended the perfect metaphor was shared. Think about a dandelion. A dandelion pops up everywhere and grows without a whole lot of support. You can see them in the middle of the sidewalk and sometimes even growing out of a building. No matter the condition, dandelions are going to thrive and grow. Most children are dandelions; they are going to thrive no matter the circumstances. Do they really need the intensive interventions to be successful?

No they don't. Orchids however are very different. They need just the right amount of sunlight and care to grow and be the exquisite flowers they are. If the slightest alteration is made to their environment it will cause them to stagger in their growth and die. Orchids represent our kids with disabilities. They are special, have the potential to be exquisite, but need the right kind of love and support to truly thrive.

I hope this book has helped to shed some light on how to best tend to the amazing orchids in your life. I cannot wait to see the type of impact they have on the world!

Sources

https://www.helpguide.org/articles/add-adhd/attention-deficit-disorder-adhd-parenting-tips.htm

http://schoolmentalhealth.org/Resources/Fam/Tips%20for%20Parents.pdf

https://www.noodle.com/articles/how-to-help-a-child-diagnosed-with-emotional-disturbance

onestops.info

pbisworld.com

addittudemag.org

understood.org

medicalnewstoday.com

kidshealth.org

mendability.com

worrywisekids.org

http://www.do2learn.com/disabilities/CharacteristicsAndStrategies/TraumaticBrainInjury_Characteristics.html

http://www.brainline.org/content/2011/10/accommodations-guide-for-students-with-brain-injury.html

http://www.do2learn.com/disabilities/CharacteristicsAndStrategies/SpeechLanguageImpairment_Strategies.html

www.mommyspeechtherapy.com

learnnc.org

https://www.thoughtco.com/behavioral-and-emotional-disorders-3110677

http://www.bcps.org/offices/special_ed/services.html

CPSIA information can be obtained
at www.ICGtesting.com
Printed in the USA
BVOW05*0437221117
500173BV00049B/295/P